Preface

Corporate governance is the system and structures of rules, practices and processes by which a company is directed and controlled, the goals and objectives of the company are established and the performance of the company is tracked. Traditionally, corporate governance has focused on the owners of the corporation that have supplied the financial capital necessary for the business to operate (i.e., the shareholders), regulation of the duties and responsibilities of the persons that the owners have selected as their agent to deploy their financial capital and generate a reasonable return on their investment (i.e., the directors and the members of the executive team); the control environment, which includes accounting procedures, internal controls and external audits used to track the operational activities of the company selected by the directors as the best means for delivering the anticipated return on investment to the shareholders; and transparency and disclosure, which are needed in order for the shareholders to fully understand how their financial capital has been used and to ensure that their agents, the directors and members of the executive team, have not abused their positions.

As time has gone by, corporate governance has emerged from what often seemed to be an esoteric collection of laws, regulations and contracts to recognition of its role as a primary driver of competitive advantage and profitability and a means for making and executing strategic decisions and ensuring that companies achieve their goals. Writing in 2008, Jamali et al. summed up the importance of corporate governance as follows:

> The importance of [corporate governance] lies in its quest at crafting/ continuously refining the laws, regulations, and contracts that govern companies' operations, and ensuring that shareholder rights are safeguarded, stakeholder and manager interests are reconciled, and that a transparent environment is maintained wherein each party is able to assume its responsibilities and contribute to the corporation's growth and value creation. Governance thus sets the tone for the organization, defining how power is exerted and how decisions are reached.[1]

In 2010, the International Finance Corporation (IFC) described corporate governance as referring "to the structures and processes for the direction and control of companies" and limited the coverage of corporate governance to the areas mentioned above (i.e., shareholders, directors, controls, transparency and disclosure). Notably, the IFC made it clear that it did not consider corporate governance to include, although the IFC said it might reinforce, corporate social responsibility (CSR) and corporate citizenship; socially responsible investing and other elements of what had become to be referred to as "corporate sustainability" such as political governance, business ethics, anti-corruption and anti-money laundering.[2] However, since that time, as the world worked its way through a global financial crisis that called into question the norms of corporate governance that had been in place since the 1970s and serious questions arose regarding the environmental and societal impacts of the decisions of shareholders and directors, there has been a clear shift in perceptions regarding the relationship between corporate governance and sustainability. In its guidance to corporate directors for 2018, one of the world's most prestigious legal advisors to boards on transactions and governance issues described the changing landscape as follows: "… while corporate governance continues to be focused on the relationship between boards and shareholders, there has been a shift toward a more expansive view that is prompting questions about the broader role and purpose of corporations … [i]n particular, sustainability has become a major, mainstream governance topic that encompasses a wide range of issues such as climate change and other environmental risks, systemic financial stability, labor standards, and consumer and product safety. Relatedly, an expanded notion of stakeholder interests that includes employees, customers, communities, and the economy and society as a whole has been a developing theme in policymaking and academic spheres as well as with investors".[3]

Corporations now operate in a world in which a shift is occurring away from the primacy of shareholder interests, which was the dominant theme of corporate governance, at least in the U.S., for decades, and toward an enlightened view of corporations as being committed to all of its stakeholders including the general economy and the community. All of this has redefined and expanded the beneficiaries of the directors' fiduciary duties beyond shareholders to other constituencies, or stakeholders, such as employees, customers, members of the local communities in which the corporation operates and society as a whole. If stakeholder primacy is accepted, as appears to be the case, albeit slowly, it opens the door for directors to consider issues and initiatives relating to sustainability, employee welfare, social concerns and environmental stewardship.

At the same time, there is strong evidence of a convergence between corporate governance and CSR/sustainability, which share many common features that are likely to promote good governance while at the same time encouraging greater attention to, and improvements in, CSR initiatives.

Convergence has influenced both public regulation and self-regulation of corporations, many of which have adopted voluntary standards, such as internal codes of conduct, relating to environmental and social responsibility, stakeholder engagement and non-financial reporting and disclosures. While these steps have been welcomed by proponents of corporate sustainability, there are some that argue that relying on corporations to "do the right thing" is not enough and that new hard laws and public regulations are needed in order to push corporations to proactively address global problems that many feel corporations help to create such as climate change, environmental degradation, exploitative labor conditions and worsening economic inequality. In addition, while financial performance has always been important to investors, many of them, particularly large public pension funds and other institutional investors, have become more interested in, and concerned about, environmental protection, human rights, health and safety, and diversity and have shown a greater appreciation for the benefits of pursuing corporate sustainability as opposed to only rewarding short-term profitability.

The new bottom line for directors is that sustainability is being recognized more and more as a strategic business question and they now need to acknowledge that sustainability is part of their corporate responsibility of guiding and overseeing corporate activities.[4] Identifying, acknowledging and addressing corporate sustainability issues creates new and significant challenges for directors and the management team that range from setting high-level goals and adopting strategies to achieve those goals to extensive changes in day-to-day operational activities. Directors must not only ensure that their companies are conducting full assessments of the entire lifecycle of their products and services but must also provide the resources and incentives to collect, analyze and report information relating to the progress of the company's corporate sustainability initiatives. Institutional investors and other stakeholders will not be satisfied with vague promises and aspirational principles from their companies, nor will companies be able to simply continue to adopt a reactive approach to sustainability-related concerns (i.e., waiting until a shareholder proposal on a sustainability topic is imminent before engaging with the shareholder to resolve the concern). In fact, directors should expect that stakeholders will demand that companies demonstrate a proactive approach to developing and implementing sustainability strategies, allocating capital to sustainability-related initiatives and effectively and transparently managing the risks associated with failure to respond to sustainability issues.

The goal of this publication is to provide directors and their professional advisors with a practical guide to a new world of corporate governance in which sustainability is front and center as a boardroom issue. In addition to further discussion of the relationship between corporate governance and sustainability and the expectations regarding board oversight of sustainability, the publication introduces the key legal and voluntary standards that directors must consider in addressing sustainability and provides valuable suggestions for creating and managing an effective sustainability governance framework including allocation of responsibilities to board committees, preparing and implementing internal governance instruments and organizing for sustainability. The publication also addresses the emergence of alternative business structures that might be better suited to social enterprise, such as benefit corporations. While most of the discussion in the publication is based on standards and practices in the U.S., we have also addressed developments in other jurisdictions and the lessons and suggestions should be valuable for companies and their advisors all around the world. The publication also includes links to sample documents that have been posted on the website of the Sustainable Entrepreneurship Project (www.seproject.org), which has been founded and operated by the author of this publication. Reference should also be made to the author's volume on *Sustainability Management*, which is being published by Routledge contemporaneously with this volume.

Notes

1 D. Jamali, A. Safieddine and M. Rabbath, "Corporate Governance and Corporate Social Responsibility Synergies and Interrelationship", *Corporate Governance*, 16(5) (2008), 443, 444 (citing J. Page, *Corporate Governance and Value Creation* (University of Sherbrooke, Research Foundation of CFA Institute, 2005)).

2 International Finance Corporation, *Corporate Governance: List of Key Corporate Governance Terms* (2010), 4.

3 M. Lipton, S. Rosenblum, K. Cain, S. Niles, V. Chanani and K. Iannone, "Some Thoughts for Boards of Directors in 2018" (Wachtell, Lipton, Rosen & Katz, November 30, 2017), 1, available at www.wlrk.com/webdocs/wlrknew/WLRKMemos/WLRK/WLRK.25823.17.pdf (accessed May 13, 2020).

4 The Global Compact LEAD, *Discussion Paper: Board Adoption and Oversight of Corporate Sustainability*.

1 Corporate Governance and Sustainability

As time has gone by, corporate governance has emerged from what often seemed to be an esoteric collection of laws, regulations and contracts to recognition of its role as a primary driver of competitive advantage and profitability and a means for making and executing strategic decisions and ensuring that companies achieve their goals. One of the most common descriptions of corporate governance has been the way that corporations are directed, administered and controlled, and the actual activities of the directors and senior executives have been referred to as steering, guiding and piloting the corporation through the challenges that arise as it pursues its goals and objectives. At the board level, the focus is on leadership and strategy and directors are expected to deliberate, establish, monitor and adjust the corporation's strategy, determine and communicate the rules by which the strategy is to be implemented, and select, monitor and evaluate the members of the senior executive team who will be responsible for the day-to-day activities associated with the strategy. In addition, directors are expected to define roles and responsibilities, orient management toward a long-term vision of corporate performance, set proper resource allocation plans, contribute know-how, expertise and external information, perform various watchdog functions, and lead the firm's executives, managers and employees in the desired direction.[1]

Setting the strategy for the corporation obviously requires consensus on the purpose of the firm, the goals and objectives of the firm's activities and the parties who are to be the primary beneficiaries of the firm's performance. Traditionally, directors were seen as the agents of the persons and parties that provided the capital necessary for the corporation to operate—the shareholders—and corporate governance was depicted as the framework for allocating power between the directors and the shareholders and holding the directors accountable for the stewardship of the capital provided by investors. While economists and corporate governance scholars from other disciplines recognized that the governance framework involved a variety of tools and mechanisms such as contracts, organizational designs and legislation, the primary question was how to use these tools and mechanisms in the best way to motivate and guarantee that the managers of the corporation would deliver a competitive rate of return.[2] All of this is consistent with what has been described as the "narrow view" of corporate governance, one that conceptualizes corporate governance as an enforced system of laws and of financial accounting, where socio/environmental considerations are accorded a low priority.[3]

For a long time, the most influential voice among academics with respect to the role and primary objective of corporations was Milton Friedman, the Nobel Prize winning economist who provided the foundation for the so-called "shareholder primacy" view of corporate governance by famously declaring that the exclusive goal of corporate activities was to maximize value for the owners of the corporation (i.e., the shareholders). As history shows, this view was seized upon by investors and CEOs who often used aggressive tactics to drive up share prices and create large, yet often dysfunctional, conglomerates. Friedman and others who shared his view maintained that companies did make a positive social contribution by running a profitable business, employing people, paying taxes and distributing some part of their net profits to shareholders.[4]

Eventually, however, other members of the academic community, as well as regulators, politicians, activists and even some of the investors that had grown wealthy during the stock market turbulence over the three decades starting with the 1980s, began to question the primacy of shareholder value and called for rethinking the role of the corporation in society and its duties to their owners and other parties impacted by their operational activities and strategic decisions. Among other things, this meant challenging the long-accepted assumption that the principal participants in the corporate governance framework were the shareholders, management and board of directors. For example, Sir Adrian Cadbury, Chair of the U.K. Commission on Corporate Governance, famously offered the following description of corporate governance and the governance framework in the Commission's 1992 Report on the Financial Aspects of Corporate Governance:

> Corporate governance is concerned with holding the balance between economic and social goals and between individual and communal goals. The governance framework is there to encourage the efficient use of resources and equally to require accountability for the stewardship of those resources. The aim is to align as nearly as possible the interests of individuals, corporations and society.

Cadbury's formulation of corporate governance brought an array of other participants, referred to as "stakeholders", into the conversation: employees, suppliers, partners, customers, creditors, auditors, government agencies, the press and the general community. The focus on interested parties beyond shareholders is the hallmark of a broader view of corporate governance that emphasizes the responsibilities of business organizations to all of the different stakeholders that provide it with the necessary resources for its survival, competitiveness and success.[5] Williams described the rationale for the stakeholder perspective to corporate governance as follows:[6]

> From a stakeholder perspective, successful companies incorporate and rely upon multiple social and natural inputs, such as an educated workforce, the physical infrastructure for the production, transportation and distribution of goods, an effective legal system, and natural capital inputs of water, air, commodities, and so forth. Since some significant portion of the inputs of corporate success, including financial inputs, have been contributed by parties other than shareholders, those parties also have interests to be considered in determining the responsibilities of managers and directors and in distributing the outputs of corporate action. Some, perhaps many, of those interests will be protected by contractual or regulatory arrangements, but others cannot be specified ex ante, and so must depend on corporate participants to fairly balance multiple parties' legitimate claims ex post.

Various countries around the world, including the U.S., have recognized alternative legal forms for for-profit social enterprises, such as benefit corporations, that explicitly expand the fiduciary duties of directors beyond maximizing shareholder value, which is still one of the primary goals of the enterprise, to include consideration of whether or not the enterprise's activities have an overall positive impact on society, its workers, the communities in which it operates and the environment. In 2019 Canada amended its business corporation statutes to integrate the holdings of that country's Supreme Court that, in evaluating the best interests of a corporation, directors could look beyond the interests of shareholders and consider the interests of a broader array of stakeholders, including employees, creditors, consumers and others. Specifically, the Canada Business Corporations Act (CBCA) now provides that when acting with a view to the best interests of the corporation, directors and officers may consider, but are not limited to, factors such as the interests of shareholders, employees, retirees and pensioners, creditors, consumers and governments; the environment; and the long-term interests of the corporation. The amendments also imposed new disclosure requirements on companies organized under the CBCA with respect to executive pay, corporate diversity and employee wellbeing.

Corporate Social Responsibility and Sustainability

The traditional profit-centered approach to management originated during the Industrial Age with the presumption that capital formation was the only legitimate role of business and that managers were obligated above all other things to pursue profits to enhance the wealth of their shareholders; however, the 1960s and 1970s saw the slow ascendency of the social responsibility approach to management which was based on the assumption that businesses were actors in a broader environment and thus had responsibilities to respond to social pressures and demands and treat their stakeholders in a manner that complied with both law and ethics.[7] Writing in the 1970s, Davis defined corporate social responsibility, or CSR, as "the firm's considerations of, and response to, issues beyond the … economic, technical, and legal requirements of the firm to accomplish social benefits along with the traditional economic gains which the firm seeks".[8] By the 1980s, the notion that corporations had a duty to behave ethically had achieved broad acceptance and attention then began to turn to what ethical behavior actually entailed, how companies should respond to business-related social issues and how "corporate social performance" should be measured. Beginning in the 1990s, a new economic theory of the firm, the "corporate community model", put stakeholders at the center of corporate strategy as partners who contributed their special knowledge to create value and competitive advantage through collaborative problem solving.[9]

In 2011 the European Commission provided a simple, yet expansive and important, definition of CSR as being "the responsibility of enterprises for their impacts on society" and went on to explain that "[e]nterprises should have in place a process to integrate social, environmental, ethical, human rights and consumer concerns into their business operations and core strategy in close collaboration with their stakeholders".[10] The World Business Council for Sustainable Development (WBCSD), an organization established and led by chief executive officers of companies focused on sustainability, has defined CSR as "the continuing commitment by business to behave ethically and contribute to economic development while improving the quality of life of the workforce and their families as well as of the local community and society at large".[11] This definition recognizes the traditional role of corporations in seeking economic benefits and then expands the responsibilities of corporations to include the voluntary pursuit, as a matter of ethical conduct as opposed to compliance with legal requirement, of wellbeing for a broad range of non-investor constituencies including employees and their families, the local communities in which the business is operated and society as a whole (e.g., environmental responsibility).

While CSR is generally associated with ensuring the corporations contribute to sustainable economic development at the macro-level, the concept of corporate sustainability can be seen as primarily concerned with the survival, or sustainability, of the corporation itself, something that is necessary in order for the corporation to make the contributions to society that are expected from being a "responsible corporate citizen". Corporate sustainability goals and programs are focused on issues that not only impact society as a whole but must also be addressed by the directors and managers of a corporation in order for it to survive and thrive: climate change; resource scarcity; demographic shifts; and regulatory and political changes.[12]

A 2017 article in *The Economist* described "sustainability" in the corporate context as follows:

> The term "sustainability" is often used interchangeably with CSR or viewed exclusively through an environmental lens. Thought leaders, however, generally describe it as a business strategy that creates long-term stakeholder value by addressing social, economic, and environmental opportunities and risks material to a company. It is integral to a company's business and culture, rather than on the periphery. Optimizing waste reduction, or water or energy consumption, for example, can help a company reduce operational costs. Sustainability can drive innovation by reconceiving products and services for low-income consumers, opening new lines of business and boosting revenue in the process. Finally, being socially responsible can help a company earn license to operate in new markets, and attract and retain talent.[13]

While the terms CSR and corporate sustainability are often used interchangeably, there are real and important distinctions between the two concepts; however, corporations can and should pursue both CSR and sustainability in order to generate the most value for all of their stakeholders:

- Avoiding environmental harm from operational activities is not only a socially responsible way to conduct business but also ensures that the corporation has sufficient natural resources available to it to survive and thrive in the future
- Monitoring the environmental and social impact of the activities of members of the corporation's supply chain not only protects natural and human resources but also ensures that the corporation will have reliable partners and a stable stream of inputs for its products
- Treating employees and their families fairly and providing them with a living wage not only enhances their wellbeing but also makes it easier for the corporation to attract and retain the talent necessary to create and commercialize innovative products and services needed to maintain long-term competitiveness
- Honest engagement with local communities and environmental and social activists promotes mutual understanding and problem solving while reducing potential distractions for directors and members of the management team
- Products that are developed in an environmentally and socially responsible manner not only reduce the burden on natural and human resources but also improve the corporation's reputation and brand and reduce the risk of consumer disenchantment and product recalls

Convergence of CSR and Corporate Governance

It has been noted that corporate governance and CSR share many common features that are likely to promote good governance while at the same time encouraging greater attention to, and improvements in, CSR initiatives.[14] Examples include regulatory approach, which is both cases has largely been based on voluntary codes and self-regulation; transparency, which has been integrated into corporate governance through reporting requirements on financial performance and now appears in connection with the voluntary disclosure and reporting on CSR initiatives and topics such as environmental, labor and human rights matters; independent directors, which have traditionally been used as a means for ensuring that the interests of shareholders are protected but could also be proponents for taking into account a broader group of stakeholder interests and could therefore play an important role in advancing CSR; greater diversity of board members, which could enhance both corporate governance and CSR; risk management, an obligation of the board of directors that has always been part of corporate governance but which has been expanded to include the risk and opportunities associated with key topics of CSR (i.e., climate change, the environment, health, safety, human rights etc.); and "whistleblowing" procedures for employees and other stakeholders that can be used to report both corporate governance and regulatory compliance problems and activities of the company that are unethical and/or likely to have adverse environmental and/or social impacts.[15]

The convergence of CSR and corporate governance has been slowly but surely evolving over a number of decades beginning with "the sophistication of consumers in the 1960s, the environmental movement of the 1970s and the increasing interest in the social impacts of business in the 1990s".[16] While these changes and movements did not always trigger specific CSR initiatives, they did set the stage along with "the global social urge to include the previously excluded social costs of production and the hidden costs incurred by the environment as a result of business activities with the corporate balance sheet; the lack of confidence in the institutions of the market economy; and the demand for ensuring sustainable development".[17] According to Rahim, the result of all this was increased pressure to update and extend the narrower meaning of corporate governance to enable companies to demonstrate their responsibility to all of their stakeholders and society in general through their performance. As time has gone by, CSR has become recognized as "[a] business strategy to make the ultimate goals of corporations more achievable as well as more transparent, demonstrate responsibility towards communities and the environment, and take the interests of groups such as employees and consumers into account when making long-term business decisions".[18]

Impact of Convergence on Corporate Regulation

Rahim observed that the potential convergence of CSR and corporate governance has affected the modes of corporate regulation and that "hierarchical command-and-control" regulation dictated by the state is being replaced by a mixture of public and private, state and market, traditional and self-regulation institutions that are based on collaboration among the state, business corporations and NGOs.[19] In fact, Rahim argued that the impact of the convergence of CSR and corporate governance has mostly been reflected by the development of self-regulatory regimes in the business environment which include both attempts by organized groups to regulate the behavior of its members and efforts by individual companies to exercise control over themselves to maintain the stability of their function and achieve certain organizational goals.[20] While self-regulation can be mandated or coerced by the state, most of the self-regulatory initiatives to date relating to CSR have been voluntary systems initiated and operated by corporations, often acting collectively with input from stakeholders. All of this seems to be consistent with the erosion of the authority and power of the nation-state that has occurred due to globalization and the accompanying rise of the influence of non-state actors and transnational bodies in constructing regulatory schemes and devices for businesses.[21]

Companies have been self-regulating their CSR-related activities through their own codes of conduct and/or through incorporation of a multi-stakeholder initiative or guidelines prepared by another social or commercial organization.[22] When corporations create their own codes of conduct they are simultaneously acting as both "regulator", responsible for the rules, and the "regulated", responsible for implementation of those rules. Acting in this fashion provides the corporation with the flexibility to frame its own internal strategies for pursuit of broader public policy goals taking into account its specific circumstances and resources. On the other hand, when corporations adopt technical and qualitative standards provided by multi-stakeholder initiatives and other external organizations, the regulator is separated from the regulated, although corporations are generally encouraged to get involved in standard-setting exercises to ensure that their concerns are heard and addressed. While acting in this manner arguably increases the costs associated with implementation and compliance, it does provide corporations with the opportunity to access emerging best practices amongst their peers and enhance their brand and reputation by being associated with widely-respected standards.

The codes of conduct referred to above began to appear during the 1990s, often adopted by large companies with a strong presence in developing economies with weak state-based regulatory systems and companies engaged in sectors where brand reputation and export orientation were critical (e.g., apparel, sporting goods, toy and retail sectors, oil, chemicals, forestry and mining).[23] In general, these codes addressed corporate ethics, moral guidelines and key CSR issues like human rights, labor, the environment and sustainable development.[24] Notably, the codes generally extended outward to include supply chain participants and included restrictions on doing business with suppliers that did not respect workers' rights (e.g., freedom of association) and ensure fair pay and treatment for their workers. Suppliers were also expected to support sustainability and use ethical practices to ensure their product quality and processing efficiency (e.g., refrain from using child labor and provide for environmentally friendly manufacturing methods). In many cases, companies supplemented their codes by providing training programs for suppliers and creating mandatory environmental management systems.[25]

Codes of conduct have been criticized as tools used by corporations to pursue their own interests rather than public policy goals and for failing to actually improve corporate behavior worldwide absent accompanying changes in business culture and decision making.[26] Companies have also been criticized for creating codes of conduct that are complex and difficult to interpret and then ignoring them in practice or failing to ensure that they are prioritized through proactive communications from the independent directors and the members of the senior executive team.[27] In turn, proponents of codes of conduct argue that the codes can positively affect sales, purchasing and recruitment of new staff, secure the company's reputation, create innovation, increase motivation among their employees and improve risk management and compliance, all of which ultimately leads to the increased sustainability of their company.[28] Codes of conduct have also been praised for their potential positive impact on internal governance including clarification of the company's mission, values and principals and their value as a guide and source of reference for the day-to-day decision making of employees.

Another feature of self-regulation has been the growing attention to non-financial reporting, a trend that began in the 1990s in response to a series of environmental disasters and continued thereafter to expand to include a wider range of corporate policies and CSR-related issues.[29] At the beginning, these reports primarily focused on informing the public of the company's existing CSR policies; however, as time went by companies began to use the reporting process as a means for creating channels of communication with their stakeholders. As this so-called "sustainability reporting" has become more sophisticated, incorporating metrics to be used to track the company's CSR performance, it has become a driver of corporate governance practices and pushes boards toward considering and incorporating better mechanisms for long-term accountability to their constituencies. While sustainability reporting has been largely voluntary, there is now a trend among legislators and regulators to require such reporting alongside traditional disclosures of financial results.

Investor Interest in CSR and Sustainability and Impact on Board Oversight

Sustainability has become an important issue for the major institutional investors and asset managers and the marketplace is seeing an increase in smaller, more specialized investment funds that are primarily oriented toward providing capital to companies that excel in their environmental, social and governance (ESG) practices and which focus on ESG-oriented activities such as climate change and impact investing.[30] The goal of these investors is to encourage their portfolio companies to contribute to the successful pursuit of environmental and social outcomes while continuing to provide investors with a suitable financial return and companies interested in attracting these types of capital providers need to pay special attention to the tools and metrics that they use for their investment decisions including negative/exclusionary screening, best-in-class positive screening, ESG integration, "impact", and business models focusing on high profile sustainability themes (e.g., cleantech, infrastructure, energy-efficient real estate or sustainable forestry).[31]

A number of factors have contributed to the surge in the interest of investors in corporate sustainability and the ESG practices of their portfolio companies:[32]

- Recognition in the financial community that ESG factors play a material role in determining risk and return
- Understanding and acceptance that incorporating ESG factors is part of investors' fiduciary duty to their clients and beneficiaries
- Concern about the impact of short-termism on company performance, investment returns and market behavior
- Increased legal requirements protecting the long-term interests of beneficiaries and the wider financial system
- Pressure from competitors seeking to differentiate themselves by offering responsible investment services as a competitive advantage
- Increasing activism of beneficiaries who are demanding transparency about where and how their money is being invested
- Concern regarding value-destroying reputational risk associated with environmental and social issues such as climate change, pollution, working conditions, employee diversity, corruption and aggressive tax strategies in a world of globalization and social media

The potential benefits to institutional investors have been highlighted by the Conference Board, which has argued that CSR enhances market and accounting performance, lowers the cost of capital, improves business reputation and fosters new revenue growth when it is channeled toward product innovation.[33] Similarly, the chairman and chief executive officer

(CEO) of BlackRock, Inc., the largest asset manager in the world, wrote in his 2016 Annual Letter to the CEOs of BlackRock's portfolio companies that "[o]ver the long-term, environmental, social and governance (ESG) issues—ranging from climate change to diversity to board effectiveness—have real and quantifiable financial impacts".[34] While many investors argue that focusing on corporate sustainability is necessary in order for companies to identify and mitigate the risks to current operations due to climate change, shortages of natural resources and ignoring basic human rights issues, investors also believe that developing and implementing innovating solutions to environmental problems, improving workplace conditions and forging strong relationships with local communities will lead to better economic performance for the business.

Investor activism around ESG issues and investors' growing demand for investment-grade ESG information has important implication for how directors should approach corporate governance, investor engagement, compliance and disclosure practices.[35] First of all, the broadened scope of risks that directors must consider in light of ESG activism means that boards must have new capacities to support oversight of ESG risk. Second, investors want their companies to integrate ESG performance metrics and long-term benchmarks into executive compensation. Third, directors need to ensure that investor engagement encourages dialogue and learning and confirm that senior management and investor relations personnel are aware of the increasing overlap between corporate governance and environmental and social concerns. Finally, directors need to improve the quality and formatting of their sustainability-related reporting and ensure that ESG materiality is being considered as part of their company's financial reporting process. Companies that can improve their practices in these areas are likely to see improved financial and operational performance, improved focus on long-term risk and return, better access to "patient capital" (i.e., investors that are less fixated on quarterly earnings and more supportive of R&D and other investments in the company's future) and be able to identify and exploit new sources of value for the company and keep ahead of emerging risks and opportunities.[36]

Transparency and Disclosure

As interest in CSR and corporate sustainability has grown, companies have found that they are subject to heightened scrutiny and that the traditional disclosure practices that focused primarily, if not exclusively, on financial information and performance and related risks are no longer adequate. Companies must now be prepared to provide disclosures that address the specific concerns and expectations of multiple stakeholders beyond investors, including customers, employees, business partners, regulators and activists. This means that the board of directors must understand existing and emerging disclosure requirements and ensure that the company has the necessary resources to collect and analyze the required information and present it in a manner that is clear and understandable. While certain CSR and corporate sustainability disclosures have now become minimum legal requirements in some jurisdictions, in general such disclosures are still a voluntary matter and directors have some leeway as to the scope of the disclosure made by their companies and how they are presented to investors and other stakeholders.

When companies were first attempting to provide voluntary disclosures relating to their CSR and corporate sustainability initiatives they often struggled with the format and depth of their reporting. Fortunately, as time went by, a consensus began to emerge about the benchmarks that companies should use for guidance in preparing their CSR and corporate sustainability reports. Of particular note are the standards for sustainability reporting developed by the Global Reporting Initiative, the International Integrated Reporting Framework developed by the International Integrated Reporting Council and the resources available from the Sustainability Accounting Standards Board; however, while the efforts of these organizations indicate that some progress has been made regarding the development of measurement and disclosure frameworks relating to corporate sustainability and ESG practices, companies and their stakeholders are not yet able to rely on universally accepted guidelines.

Notes

1 K. MacMillan, K. Money, S. Downing and C. Hillenbrad, "Giving Your Organization SPIRIT: An Overview and Call to Action for Directors on Issues of Corporate Governance, Corporate Reputation and Corporate Responsibility", *Journal of General Management*, 30 (2004), 15; A. Cadbury, "The Corporate Governance Agenda", *Journal of Corporate Governance*, Practice-Based Papers, 8 (2000), 7; and J. Page, *Corporate Governance and Value Creation* (University of Sherbrooke, Research Foundation of CFA Institute, 2005).
2 H. Mathiesen, *Managerial Ownership and Finance Performance* (Dissertation presented at Copenhagen Business School, 2002).
3 K. Saravanamuthu, "What is Measured Counts: Harmonized Corporate Reporting and Sustainable Economic Development", *Critical Perspectives on Accounting*, 15 (2004), 295.
4 C. Williams, "Corporate Social Responsibility and Corporate Governance" in J. Gordon and G. Ringe (Eds.), *Oxford Handbook of Corporate Law and Governance* (Oxford: Oxford University Press, 2016), 35, available at http://digitalcommons.osgoode.yorku.ca/scholarly_works/1784 (accessed May 10, 2020).
5 K. MacMillan, K. Money, S. Downing and C. Hillenbrad, "Giving your organization SPIRIT: An overview and call to action for directors on issues of corporate governance, corporate reputation and corporate responsibility", *Journal of General Management*, 30 (2004), 15.

6 C. Williams, "Corporate Social Responsibility and Corporate Governance" in J. Gordon and G. Ringe (Eds.), *Oxford Handbook of Corporate Law and Governance* (Oxford: Oxford University Press, 2016), 38–39, available at http://digitalcommons.osgoode.yorku.ca/scholarly_works/1784 (accessed May 10, 2020) (citing M. Blair and L. Stout, "A Team Production Theory of Corporate Law", *Virginia Law Review*, 85 (2003), 248).

7 C. Masuku, *Corporate Social Responsibility Literature Review and Theoretical Framework*, available at www.academia.edu/2172462/CORPORATE_SOCIAL_RESPONSIBILITY_LITERATURE_REVIEW_AND_THEORETICAL_FRAMEWORK (accessed May 10, 2020).

8 K. Davis, "The Case For and Against Business Assumption of Social Responsibilities", *American Management Journal*, 16 (1973), 312.

9 C. Masuku, *Corporate Social Responsibility Literature Review and Theoretical Framework*, available at www.academia.edu/2172462/CORPORATE_SOCIAL_RESPONSIBILITY_LITERATURE_REVIEW_AND_THEORETICAL_FRAMEWORK (accessed May 10, 2020) (citing W. Halal, "Corporate Community: A Theory of the Firm Uniting Profitability and Responsibility", *Strategy & Leadership*, 28(2) (2000), 10).

10 European Commission, A Renewed European Union Strategy 2011–14 for Corporate Social Responsibility, COM (2011) 681, ¶ 3.1.

11 World Business Council for Sustainable Development, *Corporate Social Responsibility: Meeting Changing Expectations*, 3, available at https://wbcsd.org (accessed May 10, 2020).

12 RobecoSAM, *Corporate Sustainability*, available at www.sustainability-indices.com (accessed May 10, 2020).

13 J. Cramer-Montes, "Sustainability: A New Path to Corporate and NGO Collaborations", *The Economist* (March 24, 2017), available at www.economist.com/node/10491124 (accessed May 10, 2020).

14 D. Szabó and K. Sørensen, "Integrating Corporate Social Responsibility in Corporate Governance Codes in the EU", *European Business Law Review*, 2013(6), 1, 5–8.

15 Id.

16 M. Rahim, *Legal Regulation of Corporate Social Responsibility: A Meta-Regulation Approach of Law for Raising CSR in a Weak Economy* (Berlin: Springer, 2013), 13, 22 (citing A. Bagić, M. Škrabalo and L. Narančić, *An Overview of Corporate Social Responsibility in Croatia* (Zagreb: Academy for Educational Development (AED), MAP Consulting Inc, 2009); and T. Pinckston and A. Carroll, "A Retrospective Examination of CSR Orientations: Have They Changed?", *Journal of Business Ethics*, 15(2) (1996), 199). See also N. Kakabadse, C. Rozuel and L. Lee-Davies, "Corporate Social Responsibility and Stakeholder Approach: A Conceptual Review", *International Journal of Business Governance and Ethics*, 1(4) (2005), 277, 279 (identifying 'consumerism' and 'corporate scandals' as the most important drivers underpinning the growth in interest and acceptance of CSR).

17 M. Rahim, *Legal Regulation of Corporate Social Responsibility: A Meta-Regulation Approach of Law for Raising CSR in a Weak Economy* (Berlin: Springer, 2013), 13, 22.

18 Id. (citing A. Gill, "Corporate Governance as Social Responsibility: A Research Agenda", *Berkeley Journal of International Law*, 26 (2008), 452).

19 Id.
20 Id.
21 Id. at 27 (citing J. Cioffi, "Governing Globalisation? The State, Law, and Structural Change in Corporate Governance", *Journal of Law and Society*, 27(4) (2000), 572).
22 Id.
23 Id. at 29 (citing H. Arthurs, "Private Ordering and Workers' Rights in the Global Economy: Corporate Codes of Conduct as a Regime of Labour Market Regulation", *Labour Law in an Era of Globalisation: Transformative Practice and Possibilities* (2005), 471; and United Nations Research Institute for Social Development, *Corporate Social Responsibility and Business Regulations: How should Transnational Corporations be Regulated to Minimise Malpractice and Improve their Social, Environmental and Human Rights Record in Developing Economies?* (2004), available at www.unrisd.org at June 29, 2010).
24 E. Wymeersch, "Corporate Governance Codes and their Implementation" (Gent University, 2006).
25 M. Rahim, *Legal Regulation of Corporate Social Responsibility: A Meta-Regulation Approach of Law for Raising CSR in a Weak Economy* (Berlin: Springer, 2013), 13, 29–30.
26 Id. at 30 (citing A. Blackett, "Global Governance, Legal Pluralism and the Decentered State: A Labour Law Critique of Codes of Corporate Conduct", *Indiana Journal of Global Legal Studies*, 8 (2000), 401; and R. Locke and M. Romis, *Beyond Corporate Codes of Conduct: Work Organisation and Labour Standards in Two Mexican Garment Factories*, MIT Sloan Research Paper No. 4617-06 (August 20, 2006)).
27 See, e.g., P. Smalera, "The Valley's Mess: Why Codes of Conduct Don't Work", *Fortune* (September 1, 2010).
28 M. Rahim, *Legal Regulation of Corporate Social Responsibility: A Meta-Regulation Approach of Law for Raising CSR in a Weak Economy* (Berlin: Springer, 2013), 13, 31.
29 Id. at 31. For further discussion of the evolution of voluntary sustainability reporting, see A. Kolk, "Sustainability, Accountability and Corporate Governance: Exploring Multinationals' Reporting Practices", *Business Strategy and the Environment*, 17(1) (2008), 1; D. Hess, "Social Reporting and New Governance Regulation: The Prospects of Achieving Corporate Accountability through Transparency", *Business Ethics Quarterly*, 17 (2007), 455, 458; and J. Elkington, "The Triple Bottom Line for 21st-Century Business, The Earthscan Reader in Business and Sustainable Development" in Richard S. Starkey and Richard Welford (Eds.), *The Earthscan Reader in Business & Sustainable Development* (London: Earthscan Publications, 2001), 20–34.
30 Investors and other stakeholders assess and grade companies and their directors and senior management teams against emerging standards that cut across three dimensions: "environmental", which focuses on how a company performs as a "steward of nature" through its policies and practices with respect to impacting climate change, sustainability, carbon footprint, water usage, pollutants and conservation; "social", which focuses on how the company manages its stakeholder relationships and includes criteria relating to non-discrimination, working conditions, gender equality, diversity and inclusivity, fair pay, health and safety and community engagement; and "governance",

which focuses on the actions of the company's leaders with respect to adhering to corporate governance principles, shareholders' rights, boardroom diversity, participation by other stakeholders, alignment of executive compensation with performance objectives, audits and internal controls and business ethics. The criteria are continuously expanding to include company's lands, manufacturing facilities, offices and transportation modalities as well as human rights due diligence. Adapted from J. Chen, "Environmental, Social, and Governance (ESG) Criteria", available at www.investopedia.com/terms/e/environmental-social-and-governance-esg-criteria.asp (accessed May 10, 2020); and S. Seiden, "Recruiting ESG Directors" (Harvard Law School Forum on Corporate Governance and Financial Regulation, October 27, 2019), available at https:// corpgov.law.harvard.edu/2019/10/27/recruiting-esg-directors/ (accessed May 10, 2020).

31 A. Krauss, P. Kruger and J. Meyer, *Sustainable Finance in Switzerland: Where Do We Stand?* (Zurich: Sustainable Finance Institute, September 2016), 15.

32 www.unpri.org/about/what-is-responsible-investment (accessed May 10, 2020).

33 M. Tonello, *Corporate Investment in ESG Practices* (The Conference Board, August 5, 2015).

34 Annual Letter from Larry Fink, Chairman and CEO, BlackRock, to CEOs (February 1, 2016), available at https://blackrock.com.

35 V. Harper Ho, *Director Notes: Sustainability in the Mainstream–Why Investors Care and What It Means for Corporate Boards* (The Conference Board, November 2017), 13–14, electronic copy available at https://ssrn.com/ abstract=3080033 (based on information available at UNPRI, Signatories, www.unpri.org/signatory-directory/).

36 Id. at 15.

2 Sustainability Standards and Instruments

Since the late 1990s there has been a proliferation of transnational, voluntary standards for what constitutes responsible corporate action, including standards that have been developed by states; public/private partnerships; multi-stakeholder negotiation processes; industries and companies; institutional investors; functional groups such as accountancy firms and social assurance consulting groups; NGOs; and non-financial ratings agencies.[1] Notable multi-sector standards initiatives have included Social Accountability 8000 and the Ethical Trading Institute, and influential multilateral initiatives have included the OECD's Guidelines for Multinational Enterprises, the ISO 26000 Corporate Responsibility standards, the UN Global Compact and the "Protect, Respect and Remedy" framework in the UN's Guiding Principles on Business and Human Rights that articulates the human rights responsibilities of states and companies.[2] Most of the corporate responsibility standards are voluntary; however, many of the topics generally included within the general subject of CSR have been addressed to some degree in domestic regulations covering labor rights, environmental and consumer protection, anti-discrimination and anti-bribery.

CSR Initiatives of Governmental or Intergovernmental Bodies

Many companies have looked to CSR initiatives of governmental or intergovernmental bodies as the foundation for creating their own CSR commitments. Instruments developed and promoted by the United Nations and the other entities referenced below are widely recognized as legitimate standards that have emerged from a careful process of deliberation and input from a wide range of stakeholders with substantial experience in identifying problems and assessing potential solutions.

United Nations Global Compact

The United Nations Global Compact (www.unglobalcompact.org/) is a voluntary initiative launched in 1999 based on CEO commitments to implement universal sustainability principles and to take steps to support United Nations goals. As of April 2020, there were over 10,000 signatories to the UN Global Compact in 166 countries, both developed and developing, representing nearly every sector and size, making it the world's most popular multi-stakeholder CSR initiative. The UN Global Compact's Ten Principles, which encompass human rights, labor, environment and anti-corruption, are derived from: the Universal Declaration of Human Rights, the International Labour Organization's Declaration on Fundamental Principles and Rights at Work, the Rio Declaration on Environment and Development and the United Nations Convention Against Corruption.

OECD Guidelines for Multinational Enterprises

The OECD Guidelines for Multinational Enterprises (http://mneguidelines.oecd.org/) are the most comprehensive set of government-backed recommendations on responsible business conduct in existence today. The governments adhering to the Guidelines, all thirty-four OECD countries and twelve non-OECD countries, aim to encourage and maximize the positive impact multinational enterprises can make to sustainable development and enduring social progress. The Guidelines were first adopted in 1976 and have been revised five times since then to ensure that they remain a leading tool to promote responsible business conduct in the changing landscape of the global economy. The most recent update in 2011 took place with the active participation of business, labor, non-governmental organizations (NGOs), non-adhering countries and international organizations. The Guidelines are part of the OECD Declaration and Decisions on International Investment and Multinational Enterprises, and provide voluntary principles and standards for responsible business conduct in areas such as employment and industrial relations, human rights, environment, information disclosure, combating bribery, consumer interests, science and technology, competition and taxation. Among other things, the Guidelines call for enterprises to take fully into account established policies in the countries in which they operate and consider the views of other stakeholders.

G20/OECD Principles of Corporate Governance

Elements of CSR, including recognition of the rights of stakeholders along with shareholders and the need for regular and transparent reporting of the corporation's governance practices and performance, found their way into the G20/OECD Principles of Corporate Governance, which among other things call on corporations to:[3]

- Protect and facilitate the exercise of shareholder rights and ensure equitable treatment of all shareholders, including minority and foreign shareholders

- Recognize the rights of stakeholders established by law or through mutual agreements and ensure that where stakeholder interests are protected by law that stakeholders have the opportunity to obtain effective redress for violation of their rights
- Encourage active cooperation between corporations and stakeholders in creating wealth, jobs and the sustainability of financially sound enterprises
- Permit mechanisms for employee participation to develop
- Ensure that stakeholders participating in the corporate governance process have access to relevant, sufficient and reliable information on a timely and regular basis and are able to freely communicate their concerns about illegal or unethical practices to the board and to the competent public authorities without compromising their rights
- Publish regular and accurate disclosure concerning the company's financial situation, performance, ownership and governance that includes, among other things:
  - company objectives and non-financial information in accordance with high quality standards including policies and performance relating to business ethics, the environment and, where material to the company, social issues, human rights and other public policy commitments
  - foreseeable risk factors including business conduct risks and risks related to the environment
  - key issues relevant to employees and other stakeholders that may materially affect the performance of the company or that may have significant impacts upon them
  - governance structures and policies, including the content of any corporate governance code or policy and the process by which it is implemented
- Implement a corporate governance framework that ensures the strategic guidance of the company, the effective monitoring of management by the board, the board's accountability to the company and the shareholders and effective disclosures and communications to stakeholders
- Ensure that the board applies high ethical standards and takes into account the interests of stakeholders through the adoption, implementation and enforcement of company-wide codes of conduct that serve as a standard for conduct by both the board and key executives and set the framework for the exercise of judgement in dealing with varying and often conflicting constituencies

International Labour Organization

The International Labour Organization (ILO) (www.ilo.org) is the only tripartite United Nations agency and brings together governments, employers and workers representatives from 187 Member States, to set labor standards, develop policies and devise programs promoting decent work for all women and men. Subjects covered by ILO standards include freedom of association, collective bargaining, forced and child labor, equality of opportunity and treatment, tripartite consultation, labor administration and inspection, employment policy, employment promotion, vocational guidance and training, employment security, wages, working time, occupational safety and health, social security, maternity protection, social policy, migrant workers, HIV/AIDS, seafarers and fishers, dock workers, indigenous and tribal peoples and other specific categories of workers. Other key ILO documents include the 2008 Declaration on Social Justice for a Fair Globalization, which expresses the universality of the Decent Work Agenda and calls for all ILO members to pursue policies based on their strategic objectives that include employment, social protection, social dialogue, and rights at work; the 1998 Declaration on Fundamental Principles and Rights at Work, which commits ILO members to respect and promote principles and rights with respect to freedom of association and the effective recognition of the right to collective bargaining, the elimination of forced or compulsory labor, the abolition of child labor and the elimination of discrimination in respect of employment and occupation; and the Tripartite Declaration of Principles Concerning Multinational Enterprises and Social Policy, which sets out principles in the fields of employment, training, conditions of work and life and industrial relations that multinational enterprises, as well as governments and employers' and workers' organizations, are recommended to observe.

International Finance Corporation

The latest version of the IFC Performance Standards on Environmental and Social Sustainability went into effect on January 1, 2012. The Performance Standards are directed toward clients, providing guidance on how to identify risks and impacts, and are designed to help avoid, mitigate and manage risks and impacts as a way of doing business in a sustainable way, including stakeholder engagement and disclosure obligations of the client in relation to project-level activities. In the case of its direct investments (including project and corporate finance provided through financial intermediaries), IFC requires its clients to apply the Performance Standards to manage environmental and social risks and impacts so that development opportunities are enhanced. Together, the Performance Standards establish standards that the client is to meet throughout the life of an investment by IFC and cover: assessment and management of environmental and social risks and impacts; labor and working conditions; resource efficiency and pollution prevention; community health, safety and security; land acquisition and involuntary resettlement; biodiversity conservation and sustainable management of living natural resources; indigenous peoples; and cultural heritage.

Principles for Responsible Investment

The Principles for Responsible Investment (www.unpri.org) calls itself the world's leading proponent of responsible investment and works to understand the investment implications of ESG factors and to support its international network of investor signatories in integrating these factors into their investment and ownership decisions. The PRI, a non-profit organization, defines "responsible investment" as an approach to investing that aims to incorporate ESG factors into investment decisions, to better manage risk and to generate sustainable, long-term returns. Environmental factors include climate change, greenhouse gas emissions, resource depletion (including water), waste and pollution and deforestation. Social factors include working conditions, including slavery and child labor; local communities, including indigenous communities; conflict; health and safety; and employee relations and diversity. Governance factors include executive pay, bribery and corruption, political lobbying and donations, board diversity and structure and tax strategy. Signatories agree to follow six principles: we will incorporate ESG issues into investment analysis and decision-making processes; we will be active owners and incorporate ESG issues into our ownership policies and practices; we will seek appropriate disclosure on ESG issues by the entities in which we invest; we will promote acceptance and implementation of the principles within the investment industry; we will work together to enhance our effectiveness in implementing the principles; and we will each report on our activities and progress toward implementing the principles.

United Nations Sustainable Development Goals

The seventeen Sustainable Development Goals (SDGs) of the 2030 Agenda for Sustainable Development were adopted by world leaders in September 2015 and went into effect on January 1, 2016. It was intended that over the fifteen year period running through 2030 the SDGs, and their accompanying 169 targets, would be universally applied to all and that countries would mobilize efforts to end all forms of poverty, fight inequalities and tackle climate change, while ensuring that no one is left behind.[4] While the SDGs are not legally binding, it is intended that national governments will be expected to take ownership and establish national frameworks for the achievement of the seventeen SDGs and that countries will have the primary responsibility for follow-up and review of the progress made in implementing the SDGs. Provisions have also been made for monitoring and review of the SDGs using a set of global indicators developed by the UN

Statistical Commission and adopted by the Economic and Social Council and the UN General Assembly. Topics addressed by the SDG including no poverty; zero hunger; good health and wellbeing; quality education; gender equality; clean water and sanitation; affordable and clean energy; decent work and economic growth; industry, innovation and infrastructure; reduced inequalities; sustainable cities and communities; responsible consumption and production; climate action; "life below water"; "life on land"; peace, justice and strong institutions; and partnerships for the goals.[5]

United Nations Human Rights Instruments

The term "human rights" was mentioned seven times in the United Nations' founding charter, making the promotion and protection of human rights a key purpose and guiding principle of the Organization. The Office of the UN High Commissioner for Human Rights (www.ohchr.org/) has lead responsibility in the UN system for the promotion and protection of human rights and supports the human rights components of peacekeeping missions in several countries, and has many country and regional offices and centers. The Universal Declaration of Human Rights (1948) was the first legal document protecting universal human rights. Together with the International Covenant on Civil and Political Rights and the International Covenant on Economic, Social and Cultural Rights, the three instruments form the so-called International Bill of Human Rights. A series of international human rights treaties and other instruments that have been adopted since 1945 have expanded the body of international human rights law including the *Guiding Principles on Business and Human Rights: Implementing the United Nations "Protect, Respect and Remedy" Framework*, which was approved in 2011[6] and has become the global standard for the respective roles and duties of states and businesses relative to human rights and been integrated as central elements of other well-known international standards such as the OECD Guidelines for Multinational Enterprises, IFC Performance Standards and ISO 26000 Social Responsibility Guidance.

Sectoral CSR Commitments

Sectoral CSR commitments emerge from collective CSR initiatives among companies and other stakeholders involved in particular business sectors and/or with a common interest in a specific social or environmental responsibility issue. Examples of sectoral CSR initiatives include the following:

- The **International Council on Mining and Metals** has developed ten principles that serve as a best-practice framework for sustainable development in the mining and metals industry (www.icmm.com/en-gb/about-us/icmm-10-principles)

- The **Sustainable Agriculture Initiative Platform** is the primary global food and drink value chain initiative for sustainable agriculture and has developed (or co-developed) tools and guidance to support global and local sustainable sourcing and agriculture practices (www. saiplatform.org/)
- The **Voluntary Principles on Security and Human Rights** (www. voluntaryprinciples.org/) are the only human rights guidelines designed specifically for extractive sector companies and are based on a collaboration of governments, companies and NGOs

International Multi-Stakeholder Processes

International multi-stakeholder processes have become a popular strategy for discussing and resolving questions and conflict relating to issues of social and environmental responsibility. Multi-stakeholder processes have been described as decision-making bodies, voluntary or statutory, comprising two or more interest groups (i.e., stakeholders) who perceive a common problem and realize their interdependence in solving it and come together to share their views and agree on strategies and activities for collectively solving the problem.[7]

AccountAbility

AccountAbility (www.accountability.org/) is a leading global organization formed in 1995 to provide innovative solutions to the most critical challenges in corporate responsibility and sustainable development and promote accountability for sustainable development. AccountAbility works with corporations, non-profits and governments to embed ethical, environmental, social and governance accountability into their organizational DNA. AccountAbility provides assurance and accountability management tools and standards through its AA1000 series, which includes the AA1000 AccountAbility Principles Standard (AA1000APS) (a framework for an organization to identify, prioritize and respond to its sustainability challenges); the AA1000 Assurance Standard (AA1000AS) (a methodology for assurance practitioners to evaluate the nature and extent to which an organization adheres to the AccountAbility Principles); and the AA1000 Stakeholder Engagement Standard (AA1000SES) (a framework to help organizations ensure stakeholder engagement processes are purpose driven, robust and deliver results).

CRT Principles for Business

One of the most interesting stakeholder-focused standards for corporate governance has been developed by the Caux Round Table (CRT) (www. cauxroundtable.org), which describes itself as an international network of principled business leaders working to promote a moral capitalism. The CRT believes that the world business community should play an important role in improving economic and social conditions and, to that end, has developed the CRT Principles for Business to embody the aspiration of principled business leadership. Noting that businesses can be powerful agents of positive social change, the CRT Principals admonish businesses that they are expected to act responsibly and demonstrate respect for the dignity and interest of its stakeholders (i.e., customers, employees, owners/investors, suppliers, competitors and communities) in their policies and actions. The following General Principles in the CRT Principles were intended to serve as a foundation for dialogue and action by business leaders in search of business responsibility and a means of implementing moral values into business decision making:

- Principle 1. The responsibilities of businesses extend beyond shareholders toward stakeholders
- Principle 2. The economic and social impact of business should be focused on innovation, justice and world community
- Principle 3. Business behavior should extend beyond the letter of the law toward a spirit of trust
- Principle 4. Respect for rules
- Principle 5. Support for multilateral trade
- Principle 6. Respect for the environment
- Principle 7. Avoidance of illicit operations

Extractive Industries Transparency Initiative

The Extractive Industries Transparency Initiative (https://eiti.org) is a multi-stakeholder initiative involving governments, businesses and civil society that has developed a global standard to promote the open and accountable management of natural resources and address the key governance issues of the oil, gas and mining sectors.

Forest Stewardship Council

The Forest Stewardship Council (FSC) (www.ic.fsc.org) is a multi-stakeholder initiative formed to promote environmentally appropriate, socially beneficial and economically viable management of the world's forests. The FSC claims to be the world's strongest certification system, in terms of global reach, robustness of certification criteria and number of businesses involved in the system. The FSC has developed regionally appropriate guidelines and standards for sustainable forest management and FSC certification is frequently required as a condition to contracting with governmental agencies.

Marine Stewardship Council

The Marine Stewardship Council (MSC) (msc.org) is an international, independent, multi-stakeholder non-profit organization established to address the problem of unsustainable fishing and safeguard seafood supplies for the future. The MSC works with scientists, fisheries, seafood producers and brands and sets credible standards for sustainable fishing and supply chain traceability. Organizations meet these standards in order to demonstrate the sustainability of their products and the blue MSC label makes it easy for everyone to choose seafood that has been caught by fisheries that care for the environment.

Social Accountability International

Social Accountability International (SAI) (www.sa-intl.org) is a non-profit organization that seeks to advance human rights at work, driven by diverse perspectives to navigating evolving labor issues. SAI works to protect the integrity of workers around the world by building local capacity and developing systems of accountability through socially responsible standards. SAI established one of the world's preeminent social standards—the SA8000® Standard for decent work, a tool for implementing international labor standards that is based on the principles of international human rights norms and which includes the following elements: child labor, forced or compulsory labor, health and safety, freedom of association and right to collective bargaining, discrimination, disciplinary practices, working hours, remuneration and management system.

Roundtable on Sustainable Palm Oil

The Roundtable on Sustainable Palm Oil (www.rspo.org) is a multi-stakeholder learning and criteria development process formed to advance the production, procurement, finance and use of sustainable palm oil products; develop, implement, verify, assure and periodically review credible global standards for the entire supply chain of sustainable palm oil; monitor and evaluate the economic, environmental and social impacts of the uptake of sustainable palm oil in the market; and engage and commit all stakeholders throughout the supply chain, including governments and consumers.

International Reporting and Management Standards

It is now widely acknowledged that best practices relating to the implementation of effective CSR practices must include a commitment to transparency and reporting on CSR-related activities and impacts to the organization's stakeholders, either as part of or in addition to any other disclosures that may be required of the organization by law or statute. In addition, CSR is like any other important strategic initiative and should be carried out pursuant to a formal sustainability management system and process that includes due diligence, development and implementation of strategic and operational goals and plans, monitoring and assessment of impacts overseen by the members of the governing body of the organization. Several of the most influential and widely used CSR-related standards that specifically address reporting and management have been developed by the Global Reporting Initiative (www.globalreporting. org); the International Integrated Reporting Council, or IIRC (www. integratedreporting.org); the Sustainability Accounting Standards Board (www.sasb.org); and the International Organization for Standardization (e.g., ISO 14001 (environmental management), ISO 9001 (quality management) and ISO 26000 (social responsibility)).[8]

Securities Exchanges and Regulators

Governments play a variety of roles in the financial system including enforcing disclosure rules and norms that facilitate the transfer of information from those in need of capital to those willing to provide capital in order to ensure that capital providers are able to make informed decisions about whether to invest or lend. One of the ways in which regulators intervene in the capital raising process is through the imposition of rules relating to corporate governance. While the public securities markets in the U.S. remain the largest and deepest in the world, there is clearly competition from other markets that are achieving extremely high levels of growth including capital markets in the Eurozone, the Asia-Pacific region and in emerging markets such as China and India, and securities exchanges and regulatory authorities in these jurisdictions have often shown global leadership in integrating corporate governance and CSR.

Global companies in Europe have been guided by the EU Commission's Green Paper on Promoting a Framework for CSR and the European Code of Conduct Regarding the Activities of Transnational Corporations Operating in Developing Economies.[9] Since 2003 EU accounting rules as stated in the EU Accounts Modernization Directive have required companies to report on environmental and labor issues "to the extent necessary" to provide investors with an accurate view of the company's financial position and the risks to that position.[10] The EU has implemented a directive that requires nearly 7,000 large companies and "public interest organizations", such as banks and insurance companies, to "prepare a nonfinancial statement containing information relating to at least environmental matters, social and employee-related matters including diversity, respect for human rights, anti-corruption and bribery matters".[11] When preparing their reports companies are expected to describe their business model and the outcomes and risks of their policies. Larger companies are also required to include and evaluate information on their supply chains, which means that smaller companies that act as suppliers to the reporting companies will need to expand their own data collection and information reporting activities even though they are not directly subject to the public reporting requirements. In addition, several stock exchanges around the world require social and/or environmental disclosure as part of their listing requirements including exchanges in Australia, Brazil, Canada, India, Singapore, South Africa and the London Stock Exchange.[12] Also, pension funds in countries such as Australia, Belgium, Canada, France, Germany, Italy, Japan, Sweden and the U.K. are required to disclose the extent to which the fund incorporates social and environmental information into their investment decisions.[13]

A number of individual countries in Europe have also taken actions driven, at least in part, by a series of resolutions adopted by the European Parliament to facilitate the development of the incorporation of CSR principles in its member economies such as, for example, requiring that companies adopt "triple bottom line" reporting on their environmental and social performance: Belgium passed legislation requiring pension fund managers to disclose the extent to which they consider ethical, social and environmental criteria in their investment policies and legislation requiring companies to report on social performance, although companies have not been forced to adhere to and comply with specific ILO conventions; France requires listed companies to disclose their impact on social and environmental issues in their annual reports and accounts; Germany requires public companies to issue reports including environmental and/or social information; and each of the Scandinavian countries have mandated publication of sustainability reports by public companies that are consistent with widely recognized frameworks such as the Global Reporting Initiative (GRI) and the UN Global Compact and which are expected to address labor issues, human rights concerns, gender equality, anti-discrimination and environmental issues.[14]

In contrast to Europe and the other countries mentioned above, the U.S. has been slower in using formal regulation to incorporate CSR into the business strategies and operations of corporations, an approach that is consistent with the preference in the U.S. for minimal legislative control of business, and has instead emphasized developing specialized organizations that set rules and standards, and provide enforcement regimes, for certain aspects of CSR including the Occupational Safety and Health Administration, Equal Employment Opportunity Commission, Consumer Product Safety Commission and the Environmental Protection Agency.[15] Areas in which the Securities and Exchange Commission (SEC) has engaged in rule-making, often with middling success due to legal challenges, or issuance of guidance on disclosures have included disclosures of environmental litigation against any government agency where a penalty of $100,000 is sought; explanation of climate risks to their future profitability, either from physical changes associated with climate change, or from regulatory initiatives designed to mitigate climate risk; disclosure of the ratio of the CEO's total pay to the median employee pay; mine safety disclosure; "conflict minerals" disclosure where tin, tantalum, tungsten or gold from the Democratic Republic of the Congo or neighboring countries were incorporated into listed companies' products; and "publish what you pay" transparency disclosure for extractive company payments to host countries.[16]

Notes

1 C. Williams, "Corporate Social Responsibility and Corporate Governance" in J. Gordon and G. Ringe (Eds.), *Oxford Handbook of Corporate Law and Governance* (Oxford: Oxford University Press, 2016), 7, available at http:// digitalcommons.osgoode.yorku.ca/scholarly_works/1784 (accessed May 11, 2020).

2 Id. at 8–9. See also the appendices to P. Hohnen (Author) and J. Potts (Editor), *Corporate Social Responsibility: An Implementation Guide for Business* (Winnipeg CAN: International Institute for Sustainable Development, 2007), which includes a list of national CSR guidance and suggestions for further reading.

3 Organisation for Economic Co-operation and Development, *G20/OECD Principles of Corporate Governance* (Paris: OECD Publishing, 2015) available at http://dx.doi.org/10.1787/9789264236882-en (accessed May 11, 2020).

4 For further information see www.un.org/sustainabledevelopment/sustainable-development-goals/.

5 For discussion of each of the Goals, see A. Gutterman, *Sustainability Standards and Instruments* (New York: Business Experts Press, 2020). See also www.un.org/sustainabledevelopment/sustainable-development-goals/.

6 See www.ohchr.org/Documents/Publications/GuidingPrinciplesBusinessHR_EN.pdf

7 P. Hohnen (Author) and J. Potts (Editor), *Corporate Social Responsibility: An Implementation Guide for Business* (Winnipeg CAN: International Institute for Sustainable Development, 2007), 49–50.

8 For further discussion of reporting and management standards, see A. Gutterman, *Sustainability Standards and Instruments* (New York: Business Experts Press, 2020). See also www.un.org/sustainabledevelopment/sustainable-development-goals/.

9 For further information, see http://ec.europa.eu/growth/industry/corporate-social-responsibility_en.

10 C. Williams, "Corporate Social Responsibility and Corporate Governance" in J. Gordon and G. Ringe (Eds.), *Oxford Handbook of Corporate Law and Governance* (Oxford: Oxford University Press, 2016), 14, available at http:// digitalcommons.osgoode.yorku.ca/scholarly_works/1784 (accessed May 11, 2020).

11 See ¶ 6 of Directive 2014/95/EU of the European Parliament and of the Council of 22 October 2014, amending Directive 2013/34/EU as regards disclosure of non-financial and diversity information by certain large undertakings and groups, Official Journal of the European Union L330/1–330/9.

12 C. Williams, "Corporate Social Responsibility and Corporate Governance" in J. Gordon and G. Ringe (Eds.), *Oxford Handbook of Corporate Law and Governance* (Oxford: Oxford University Press, 2016), 16, available at http:// digitalcommons.osgoode.yorku.ca/scholarly_works/1784 (accessed May 11, 2020) (citing Initiative for Responsible Investment, *Corporate Social Responsibility Disclosure Efforts by National Governments and Stock Exchanges* (March 12, 2015), available at http://hausercenter.org/iri/wpcontent/uploads/ 2011/08/CR-3-12-15.pdf). The listing rules for the Singapore Exchange, for example, require every listed company to prepare an annual sustainability report on its sustainability practices on a "comply or explain" basis with reference to five primary components: material ESG factors; policies, practices and performance; targets; sustainability reporting framework; and board statement. "SGX Sustainability Reporting Guide" in *Sustainability Guide for Boards: At a Glance* (Singapore Institute of Directors, KPMG and SGX, September 2017).

13 Id.

14 M. Rahim, *Legal Regulation of Corporate Social Responsibility: A Meta-Regulation Approach of Law for Raising CSR in a Weak Economy* (Berlin: Springer, 2013), 13, 34–38; C. Williams, "Corporate Social Responsibility and Corporate Governance" in J. Gordon and G. Ringe (Eds.), *Oxford Handbook of Corporate Law and Governance* (Oxford: Oxford University Press, 2016), 14–15, available at http://digitalcommons.osgoode.yorku.ca/scholarly_works/ 1784 (accessed May 11, 2020).

15 Id. at 38–39.

16 C. Williams, "Corporate Social Responsibility and Corporate Governance" in J. Gordon and G. Ringe (Eds.), *Oxford Handbook of Corporate Law and Governance* (Oxford: Oxford University Press, 2016), 17–18, available at http:// digitalcommons.osgoode.yorku.ca/scholarly_works/1784 (accessed May 11, 2020). Several of the topics were placed on the agenda as part of the Dodd-Frank Wall Street Reform and Consumer Protection Act of 2010; however, the rules relating to "conflict minerals" disclosure and "publish what you pay" drew strong challenges from the National Association of Manufacturers and the American Petroleum Institute and, in fact, attempts to enforce "publish what you pay" have effectively been abandoned by the SEC.

3   Board Oversight of Sustainability

The role of corporations and other business organizations in society has become a hotly debated issue that has attracted the attention of numerous participants in the political arena; however, until recently board members generally showed little interest in the debate and remained focused on their traditional role of maximizing shareholder value. It is now becoming clear that questions regarding the role of business are tied to essential strategic and operational sustainability-related issues that are critical to the discharge of directors' responsibilities with respect to setting the long-term strategy of their companies and which have attracted the attention of investors, consumers and other stakeholders upon which companies depend for their survival.

One of the most significant drivers of enhanced board oversight of sustainability has been the changing expectations of institutional investors. The consensus today among institutional investors is that "corporate sustainability" is no longer limited to the environmental practices of the company, but should be broadly construed to include all of the challenges that should be overcome—economic, environmental and social—and all of the actions that should be taken in order for the corporation's business model to survive and thrive currently and into the future. In addition, directors have become keenly aware of the expectations of other stakeholders regarding the role and purpose of corporations in society and the need for corporations, through their boards and senior executives, to forge a strategy that takes into account the environmental and social impact of operations as well as traditional financial performance objectives. Consumers are demanding that companies integrate sustainability into their products and services and employees are seeking to work for companies that aim to "make a difference" as well as profits. Lawmakers are imposing additional sustainability-related legal and regulatory compliance requirements on corporations, thus causing directors to make appropriate changes to their enterprise risk management processes. Finally, traditional notions of directors' fiduciary duties, which assumed primacy of shareholders' interests and maximizing shareholder value, are giving way to a model of directors' duties that gives due weight to the interests of stakeholders.

Identifying, acknowledging and addressing corporate sustainability issues create new and significant challenges for directors and the management team that range from setting high-level goals and adopting strategies to achieve those goals to extensive changes in day-to-day operational activities. Directors must not only ensure that their companies are conducting full assessments of the entire lifecycle of their products and services but must also provide the resources and incentives to collect, analyze and report information relating to the progress of the company's corporate sustainability initiatives. Institutional investors and other stakeholders will not be satisfied with vague promises and aspirational principles from their companies, nor will companies be able to simply continue to adopt a reactive approach to ESG-related concerns (i.e., waiting until a shareholder proposal on an ESG topic is imminent before engaging with the shareholder to resolve the concern). In fact, directors should expect stakeholders to demand that companies demonstrate a proactive approach to developing and implementing sustainability strategies, allocating capital to sustainability-related initiatives and managing the risks associated with failure to respond to ESG issues.

Directors' Adoption and Oversight of Corporate Sustainability

CSR and corporate sustainability are like any other important management initiatives and require proactive leadership from the top of the organization. In fact, it is clear that the "tone at the top" is an important factor in the success or failure of any CSR or corporate sustainability initiative and the directors and senior executives of the corporation are uniquely positioned to act as external and internal champions of CSR and corporate sustainability and proactively communicate with everyone involved with the organization on a daily basis about the impact of new environmental and socially responsible products and services. The directors and senior executives must also commit to investing the time and effort necessary to explain the corporation's CSR and corporate sustainability initiatives to customers and other stakeholders and develop and implement metrics for tracking and reporting progress. While environmental and social responsibility certainly extends "beyond the law", directors and officers must be mindful of their fiduciary duties and understand how laws, regulations and standard contract provisions are rapidly evolving to incorporate environmental and social responsibility standards.

Global Compact LEAD suggested there were five key dimensions central to the intersection of sustainability and governance: board roles and responsibilities; board structure; board composition; board engagement with investors; and sustainability education for board members.[1] KPMG recommended that directors follow a framework for board oversight of ESG issues and related strategy that includes the following parts or elements: agreeing on a definition of ESG and its importance to the company and a common language that can be used throughout the organization; conducting an assessment to identify ESG risks and opportunities and determine which are of strategic significance to the company; encouraging integration of the most strategically significant ESG issues identified in the assessment into the company's long-term business strategy and helping to ensure alignment and buy-in across the enterprise through the right culture and incentives; shaping the company's key ESG messages, its "ESG story", to investors and other stakeholders in the context of strategy and long-term value creation; and ensuring the board has the right composition, skills, structure, information and processes to oversee ESG in the context of strategy and long-term value creation.[2]

Ceres recommended that directors should ensure that sustainability issues are considered systematically in the course of the company's standard governance processes by integrating sustainability into board systems and processes, which means focusing on company-specific "material" sustainability that significantly impact operations and revenues; embedding sustainability in committee charters; regularly and continuously discussing strategy, risks and incentives; recruiting diverse candidates with expertise and backgrounds on key sustainability issues and offering sustainability training; and involving key staff responsible for enterprise profit and loss in board deliberations on sustainability.[3] Ceres also called on directors to take advantage of opportunities for action relating to sustainability including embedding sustainability and longer-term thinking into strategic planning; integrating sustainability in risk oversight; engaging with external stakeholders; establishing stronger linkages between executive compensation and sustainability goals; and disclosing the role of the board and its oversight in prioritizing sustainability in the company's reporting and communications programs.

The focus on sustainability has extended the traditional roles and responsibilities of directors and created new ones.[4] Many agree that CSR principles are typically embedded into governance practices such as disclosure and reporting, risk management oversight, board composition and diversity and compensation. Disclosure and reporting on social, environmental and ethical issues has become commonplace among larger companies and has expanded to include specific details on policy implementation and stakeholder engagement. In addition, the main standards developed for non-financial reporting, such as the GRI, have incorporated several disclosure items relating to the internal governance framework including the independence and expertise of directors; board-level processes for overseeing the identification and management of economic, environmental and social risks and opportunities, and the linkage between executive compensation and achievement of financial and non-financial goals. Risk management is a fundamental duty of the board and CSR encourages directors to take a broad view of the challenges that their companies face in maintaining performance and surviving in the marketplace. The growing emphasis on

CSR also means that boards need to be able to draw on the skills, knowledge and experiences of a more diverse group of members, a requirement that is consistent with calls for better gender and ethnicity diversity in the boardroom. Finally, boards need to develop new compensation and rewards systems that take CSR into account and prioritize metrics and success indicators that are broadly defined from a longer-term perspective.[5] All in all, as boardroom focus on sustainability has increased, directors are expected to become more involved in integration of strategy and sustainability; paying attention to stakeholder perspectives and engagement; overseeing the production of, and approving, sustainability reports; and ensuring that management is appropriately accountable for sustainability performance, and compensated properly in light of that performance.[6]

Directors' Fiduciary Duties

The primacy of shareholder interests has been the dominant theme of corporate governance, at least in the U.S., for decades, and this has complicated efforts of directors to authorize sustainability initiatives that, by their very nature, are intended to create benefits for stakeholders other than stockholders that may well adversely impact stockholder value, at least in the short term, and deprive stockholders of distributions of surplus profits.[7] However, as time has gone by, support has developed and increased for what Hart and Zingales referred to as the "constituency theory" of governance, which would expand the beneficiaries of the directors' fiduciary duties beyond shareholders to other constituencies, or stakeholders, such as employees, customers, members of the local communities in which the corporation operates and society as a whole.[8] While sentiment for encouraging long-termism and promoting a broader range of stakeholder interests has been around in some form for decades, the attacks on the primacy of shareholder value creation have never been as strident and are likely to accelerate in the future and become a permanent fixture among governance issues. Given the growing consensus that the support and goodwill of a variety of stakeholders—employees, customers, suppliers, regulators and local communities in which the company operates—is critical to the long-term success of the company, there is a compelling argument to be made that paying due consideration to the interests and concerns of the company's most important stakeholders is consistent with directors' fiduciary duties to enhance the company's long-term value.[9]

Compelling evidence of the desire to free directors of historical constraints, and thus promote more aggressive and entrepreneurial sustainability efforts, has been the decision of politicians in a majority of the states and the District of Columbia to endorse and formalize the constituency theory by adopting statutes that permit the formation of "benefit corporations", a new form of for-profit corporation that explicitly expands the fiduciary duties of directors beyond maximizing shareholder value, which is still one of the primary goals of a corporation, to include consideration of whether or not the corporation's activities have an overall positive impact on society, their workers, the communities in which they operate and the environment.[10] While the rate of adoption of benefit corporation status has been slow, particularly among public companies, the recognition of benefit corporations has contributed to sharpened focus on the separate interests of non-shareholder stakeholders and created a host of new issues and challenges for directors of all types of corporations such as how to measure and compare non-financial performance aspects of corporate activities; how to hold corporations accountable to stakeholders who do not have the rights to vote that are held by shareholders; and how to structure incentive packages for executives and managers tied to complex multi-stakeholder goals and commitments.

Framework for Board Oversight of CSR and Corporate Sustainability

CSR and corporate sustainability are broad and challenging topics and the directors must carefully consider how the board's duties and responsibilities will be discharged and allocated among board members. According to KPMG, the structure and processes a board creates to oversee CSR and corporate sustainability will vary based on a number of factors, such as the size and complexity of the company's operations (including its supply chain and whether operations are international), its industry, the magnitude of the company's CSR risks and opportunities, the degree to which CSR issues are central to the company's strategy, and the level of director expertise regarding relevant CSR issues.[11] One well-known corporate governance advisor has counseled that directors should begin the process of developing an oversight framework for CSR and corporate sustainability by asking and answering the following questions:[12]

- How should concerns regarding CSR and corporate sustainability be integrated into the board's discussions on strategy and risk oversight? Strategy and risk oversight are two topics that all board members should be working on and actively discussing during each board meeting and investors are looking to see whether CSR and corporate sustainability have been formalized as priorities in the board's governance guidelines and overall goals.
- To what extent should CSR and corporate sustainability topics be included as standalone agenda items for board meetings?
- What information should be provided to directors (e.g., data on how the company's efforts compare to those of its peer companies, leading industry standards, and the CSR-related priorities of key shareholders and proxy advisory firms)?

- Which metrics should the board and members of the executive team focus on in considering progress against CSR and corporate sustainability goals (e.g., goals involving reduction of water usage and emissions, reducing on-the-job injuries and employee turnover, or improving workforce diversity and employee retention)?
- What process should be used for drafting and reviewing public disclosures about the company's CSR and corporate sustainability efforts?

In addition, the board should also consider how the company's current efforts and activities with respect to CSR and corporate sustainability compare to its peers, how investors and other stakeholders perceive the company's engagement with and disclosure of CSR and corporate sustainability and whether or not the company has been effectively communicating its CSR and corporate sustainability strategies, goals and actions to investors and other stakeholders.[13]

The entire board also needs to consider whether it has the full team and resources necessary to effectively and credibly carry out its oversight responsibilities. For example, consideration needs to be given to the following issues and questions:[14]

- Does the board have a sufficient number of members to staff the requisite standing and special committees and to meet expectations of investors and other stakeholders with respect to diversity and ability to effectively engage with stakeholders? Institutional investors have expectations regarding director age, diversity and periodic refreshment that need to be understood and respected and the CSR and corporate sustainability pronouncements from the board will not be seen as credible unless board composition demonstrates a commitment to diversity and stakeholder representation.
- Does the board include directors who have knowledge of, and experience with, the company's businesses? While there has been a substantial wave toward including "independent" directors on boards in recent years, and this remains good advice, boards should consider adding more than one director who is not "independent" when and if that person can provide the outside directors with insight into the day-to-day operations of the business. Given that the CEO is already a member of the board, other inside directors, typically drawn from the senior executive team, must have the experience, reputation and confidence to provide views that may differ from those offered by the CEO.
- Are all of the directors able to devote sufficient time to preparing for and attending board and committee meetings? Being an effective director requires a substantial commitment of time and physical and mental resources and each director must be able to fully participate and engage in the difficult debates that continuously occur at full board

meeting and during committee meetings. Boards can no longer afford to have ceremonial directors appointed for public relations purposes, particularly when the institutional investors and other stakeholders are closely monitoring reports on director attendance and participation. Also important to consider is the time expected of each director to participate in stakeholder engagement and relationship building and education and training.

- Does the board have processes in place to ensure that directors receive all of the data, presented in a clear and objective manner, which is critical for them to be able to make sound decisions on strategy, compensation and capital allocation? Directors cannot rely solely on reports prepared by the CEO to make their decisions as fiduciaries for investors and other stakeholders, but must instead ensure that objective data is collected and analyzed through the company's internal controls and made available to directors well in advance of meetings. Data requirements should be sorted out in advance between directors and management when discussing and adopting key performance indicators for each CSR initiative and program.
- Does the board have procedures in place to ensure that directors receive continuous training and education on the rapidly expanding list of topics that will appear on the board's agenda? Directors should ensure that they are provided with regular tutorials by internal and external experts as part of expanded director education and the curriculum must cover each of the key topics that must be addressed from a CSR and corporate sustainability perspective including issues such as climate change and supply chain management and processes such as stakeholder engagement and disclosure/reporting.

Board Committees

While the entire board should consider the questions posed above, and CSR and corporate sustainability will need to have an important place on the agenda for full board meetings, larger companies typically rely on one or more committees when it comes to allocating specific tasks and tapping into specialized resources and expertise. Surveys have found that boards generally choose from among three models for formal structures relating to consideration of sustainability issues: (1) tasking the entire board with oversight, (2) creating new committees dedicated exclusively to sustainability and (3) using existing committees to assume responsibility for sustainability as one aspect of their overall activities.[15]

One approach that is growing in popularity is the creation of public policy/CSR, social and cultural responsibility and/or environmental responsibility, health, safety and technology committees composed of a sub-group of the entire board that is charged with focusing more time and effort on sustainability generally and important topics within sustainability.

Establishing a standalone committee at the board level focusing on sustainability significantly increases the amount of time that board members can dedicate to these discussions and increases the visibility of the board's commitment, thus sending an important signal to both internal and external stakeholders; however, boards need to be careful that relying on a separate committee reduces the uptake of sustainability by all of the directors and hampers integration into other functional committees. As time goes by the role of the committee will evolve to that of a "coordinator", with strategies, commitments and targets being set by the entire board and the committee providing support with the assistance of an internal sustainability office.[16]

In addition, other committees may be asked to provide support relating to specific CSR and corporate sustainability topics that are closely related to their regular activities, although it is important to avoid too much dilution of effort by making sure that the actions and activities of all committees are coordinated and the results reported upward to the entire board during the portion of the board meetings allocated to the consideration of CSR and corporate sustainability. For example, the nominating committee can contribute to the socially responsible profile of the company by ensuring that the board is diverse and represents all the company's key constituencies and that members have skills and experience necessary to engage effectively with stakeholders regarding CSR and corporate sustainability and to identify and manage risks. The governance committee should ensure that CSR, corporate sustainability and the specific issues and topics included therein are given a place on the board's education agenda. Sustainability topics should also be integrated into the activities of the compensation committee (e.g., tying executive compensation to performance on sustainability metrics) and the disclosure and reporting committee (e.g., oversight of preparation of sustainability reports and other disclosures of non-financial information). Each member of the board should be mindful of the role that he or she is expected to play with respect to CSR and corporate sustainability oversight and it is important to be clear which committees each board member will serve on and to be sure that the skills of each director are properly aligned with the internal organizational of the board.

Board Composition

Along with finding the appropriate structure for oversight of sustainability, boards must address the composition of the director team to ensure that it both demonstrates certain key values associated with social responsibility and includes members with the appropriate sustainability mindset and skills required to execute on sustainability commitments. Important issues and characteristics for board composition relative to sustainability are independence (i.e., separating the chief executive and chairperson positions and recruiting external directors), diversity (i.e., gender diversity, which has led to imposition of quotas to remedy under-representation of women on corporate boards, and including representatives of key foreign markets as companies globalize their operations), stakeholder representation (i.e., a director elected to the board specifically to represent the interests and perspectives of non-investor stakeholders, a concept that admittedly has yet to be widely adopted apart from a handful of jurisdictions with "dual board" corporate governance structures), cultures, age and viewpoints, each of which has a clear relationship to sustainability.[17]

Directors should also not underestimate the importance of diversity in the boardroom to institutional investors, many of which, such as BlackRock, have made it clear that they intend to engage with their portfolio companies to better understand their progress on improving gender balance and hold the nominating and/or governance committees of the boards of those companies responsible for any apparent lack of commitment to board effectiveness.[18] In addition, the stakes surrounding boardroom diversity took an interesting turn on September 30, 2018 when California made history by becoming the first state to mandate a minimum number of women directors for publicly held corporations headquartered in the state.[19]

Other factors are also in play that may ultimately lead to changes regardless of the fate of initiatives such as the California legislation. Studies indicate that companies are becoming increasingly concerned about their image and reputation and that taking aggressive and transparent steps to change their experiences, skill sets and life views is an important way to signal that attention is being paid to societal changes and expectations. Perceived failures in board oversight of corporate culture that has led to high profile disclosures of sexual harassment and other forms of discrimination in the workplace are also relevant. Another consideration is how decisions are actually made in boardrooms and what steps can be taken to improve decision making including incorporating the views of women and other groups that have traditionally not been part of those deliberations. Gender diversity in the boardroom and among executive teams will also be important for companies looking to become and remain more innovative, find ways to capitalize on new technologies and anticipate how technology and changes in societal values will impact the workforce.

Sustainability Education and Training for Board Members

In addition to seeking out board members with specific experience and skills relevant to sustainability, companies must ensure that all of their directors are continuously educated on sustainability in general as well as the subtopics of sustainability that are the foundation of the company's goals and commitments. Director education and training in sustainability is important for several reasons. First, directors who are unable to recognize and respond to sustainability issues are derelict in their duties with respect to risk management since those issues pose a substantial risk to the company's reputation, brand and license-to-operate. Second, directors need to understand sustainability in order to properly select and oversee senior leadership to ensure that a "culture of sustainability" is created and maintained from the very top of the organization. Finally, directors are responsible for the long-term strategy and direction of the company and in discharging those duties and making leadership decisions they need to understand how strategic management of sustainability and innovation can improve business performance.[20] Sustainability training is often assigned to the board's nominating and governance committee, which will be responsible for determining the curriculum and identifying internal faculty members and external training providers such as universities with expertise in various sustainability issues.

Notes

1 The Global Compact LEAD, *Discussion Paper: Board Adoption and Oversight of Corporate Sustainability.*

2 *ESG, Strategy and the Long View: A Framework for Board Oversight* (KPMG LLP, 2017), 2–3, 20.

3 *View from the Top: How Corporate Boards Can Engage on Sustainability Performance* (Ceres, 2015) (as cited and included in R. Sainty, "Engaging boards of directors at the interface of corporate sustainability and corporate governance", *Governance Directions* (March 2016), 85, 87).

4 For further discussion of roles and responsibilities of directors, see "Directors' Rights, Duties and Liabilities" in A. Gutterman, *Corporate Governance: An Introduction to Theory and Practice* (Oakland CA: Sustainable Entrepreneurship Project, 2019) available at www.seproject.org.

5 C. Strandberg, *The Convergence of Corporate Governance and Corporate Social Responsibility: Thought-Leaders Study* (Canadian Co-operative Association, March 2005), 9–10.

6 The Global Compact LEAD, *Discussion Paper: Board Adoption and Oversight of Corporate Sustainability.*

7 For further discussion of fiduciary duties of directors, see "Directors' Rights, Duties and Liabilities" in A. Gutterman, *Corporate Governance: An Introduction to Theory and Practice* (Oakland CA: Sustainable Entrepreneurship Project, 2019) available at www.seproject.org.

8 O. Hart and L. Zingales, "Should a Company Pursue Shareholder Value?" (October 2016), available at www8.gsb.columbia.edu/leadership/sites/leadership/files/Zingales-Hart–Share_value.pdf

9 *A New Agenda for the Board of Directors: Adoption and Oversight of Corporate Sustainability* (Global Compact LEAD, 2012), 6.

10 By 2020, over forty states and the District of Columbia had either adopted legislation authorizing the creation of a benefit corporation or were seriously considering such legislation available at https://benefitcorp.net/policymakers/state-by-state-status (accessed May 12, 2020).

11 *ESG, Strategy and the Long View: A Framework for Board Oversight* (KPMG LLP, 2017), 18.

12 H. Gregory, "Corporate Social Responsibility, Corporate Sustainability and the Role of the Board", Practical Law Company (July 1, 2017), 3.

13 D. Kuprionis and P. Styles, "Translating Sustainability into a Language Your Board Understands", *The Corporate Governance Advisor*, 25(5) (September/October 2017), 13, 15.

14 Adapted from M. Lipton, S. Rosenblum, K. Cain, S. Niles, V. Chanani and K. Iannone, "Some Thoughts for Boards of Directors in 2018" (Wachtell, Lipton, Rosen & Katz, November 30, 2017), available at www.wlrk.com/webdocs/wlrknew/WLRKMemos/WLRK/WLRK.25823.17.pdf.

15 *A New Agenda for the Board of Directors: Adoption and Oversight of Corporate Sustainability* (Global Compact LEAD, 2012).

16 *A New Agenda for the Board of Directors: Adoption and Oversight of Corporate Sustainability* (Global Compact LEAD, 2012), 14.

17 Id. at 12. See also S. Seiden, "Recruiting ESG Directors" (Harvard Law School Forum on Corporate Governance and Financial Regulation, October 27, 2019), https://corpgov.law.harvard.edu/2019/10/27/recruiting-esg-directors/ (providing recommendations on recruiting "ESG talent" for director positions including eliminating director age maximums that arbitrarily eliminate otherwise valuable candidates with unique sustainability-related expertise related to long periods of focus on relevant issues and accepting "newbies" (i.e., people who have never served on a public board) with relevant experience drawn from a pool that includes non-CEOs who are either part of the C-suite or report into the C-suite, high ranking former government or military officials, non-profit CEOs, academic officers and faculty and others with the right combination of expertise and emotional intelligence to thrive and lead (not just get along) in the boardroom).

18 *ESG, Strategy and the Long View: A Framework for Board Oversight* (KPMG LLP, 2017), 6.

19 The controversial law added Section 301.3 to the California Corporations Code, which requires that a domestic general corporation or foreign corporation that is a publicly held corporation (i.e., a corporation with outstanding shares listed on a major United States stock exchange) whose principal executive offices, according to the corporation's Securities and Exchange Commission Form 10-K, are located in California must have a minimum of one female (defined as an individual who self-identifies her gender as a woman, without regard to the individual's designed sex at birth) on its board of directors no later than December 31, 2019.

20 The Global Compact LEAD, *Discussion Paper: Board Adoption and Oversight of Corporate Sustainability*.

4   Governance and Nominating Committee

Corporate governance begins with the board of directors, regardless of the size of the corporation and any other rules to which the corporation may be subject due to its status as a "public company". Fulfillment of the duties and responsibilities of the board of directors with respect to compliance with corporate governance regulations and principles is typically led by a board-level governance and nominating committee. One of the most important activities in the governance framework is identifying and selecting qualified directors and the governance and nominating committee is the primary source of nominees to join the board. Most small venture-backed companies use the entire board as the nominating committee since board composition and recruitment have become so standardized among those types of firms. However, once a company has gone public and the founders and venture capitalists slowly leave the board, recruiting quality board members becomes a more important task that the committee takes on by developing director qualification guidelines and procedures for vetting of potential candidates. Once directors are on board the committee provides orientation and ongoing training and organizes annual evaluations of the performance of individual directors and the entire board, as well as members of the senior management team. The governance and nominating committee also makes a substantial impact with respect to committee composition, structure and function; governance policies and practices; and shareholders' proposals and engagement. With respect to sustainability, the committee should be at the forefront of efforts to incorporate sustainability into the board's oversight responsibilities, expand stakeholder engagement and diversify the composition of the board.

The New York Stock Exchange (NYSE) requires that companies establish a nominating/corporate governance committee composed of independent directors.[1] For its part, Nasdaq does not require that companies have a nominating/corporate governance committee; however, there must be "independent director" oversight of director nominations of Nasdaq-listed companies, which means that director nominees must be selected, or recommended for the board's selection, either by independent directors constituting a majority of the board's independent directors in a vote in which only independent directors participate, or by a nominations committee comprised solely of independent directors.[2] The primary purposes of these types of committees are identifying individuals that are qualified to become board members and selecting, or recommending that the board select, the nominees for election at the annual meeting of shareholders; and the development, and recommendation to the board, of a set of corporate governance principles. The NYSE requires that the committee has the sole authority, supported by adequate funding, to retain and dismiss outside advisors that may provide consulting services in connection with the committee's responsibilities, such as search firms used to identify board and management candidates. As is the case with the audit and compensation committees, the nominating/corporate governance committee must conduct an annual evaluation of its performance and should also conduct an evaluation of board and management performance no less frequently than annually.

Qualifications of Directors

The charter documents, as well as applicable corporation or company law provisions, may prescribe qualifications for directors, and reference must also be made to regulatory standards that dictate that the composition of the board comply with "independence" requirements and that directors be familiar with financial reporting and accounting rules and procedures. The board of directors, working as a group and through its governance and nominating committee, should develop a set of director qualifications that address the appropriate skills, perspectives, experiences and characteristics required of board candidates, taking into account the company's needs and the then-current makeup of the board. The qualifications should include knowledge and experience in areas critical to understanding the company and its business; technical, business and interpersonal skills; personal characteristics, such as integrity and judgment; and candidates' commitments to the boards of other publicly held companies and other outside activities. Each board member is expected to ensure that other existing and planned future commitments do not materially interfere with the member's service as a director and that he or she devotes the time necessary to discharge his or her duties as a director.

The qualification guidelines should also address the overall goals and objectives regarding diversity and optimal size and composition of the board and its various committees and, of course, applicable requirements of the securities exchanges. Directors should not underestimate the important of diversity in the boardroom to institutional investors, many of which, such as BlackRock, have made it clear that they intend to engage with their portfolio companies to better understand their progress on improving gender balance and hold the nominating and/or governance committees of the boards of those companies responsible for any apparent lack of commitment to board effectiveness.[3]

Finally, the qualification guidelines should include a brief summary of the steps taken to identify, evaluate and select candidates for board membership, including a schedule or timetable to ensure that sufficient time is allocated for the important steps of assessing the needs of the board, identifying appropriate candidates and providing them with information regarding the company and the board and, ultimately, interviewing candidates in order to gather sufficient information for the board to make a decision regarding which candidates should be nominated for the board. The governance and nominating committee should be responsible for periodically reviewing and modifying, as appropriate, the qualification guidelines.

Independence Requirements

The Sarbanes-Oxley Act of 2002 (SOX), and the supporting rules and regulations of the exchanges, require that "independent directors" comprise a majority of the board and that provision must be made for regular meetings of the independent directors in executive session.[4] In addition, the compensation of the CEO and other executive officers, as well as director nominations, must be approved by the independent directors. Both the NYSE and Nasdaq allow such approvals to be given by compensation committees composed solely of independent directors and, in fact, the NYSE requires that companies have such committees.[5] Nasdaq-listed companies are required to have a standing compensation committee comprised of at least two members and all members of the compensation committee need to be "independent directors"; however, Nasdaq does permit one non-independent director to serve on a compensation committee composed of at least three members for a limited period of time in "exceptional and limited circumstances" if certain conditions are satisfied.[6]

Many companies have integrated those rules and regulations into a set of director qualification guidelines that include not only "independence", but also characteristics that the company believes are suitable for its directors. For example, these guidelines might refer to strong management experience with a company of similar size and engaged in comparable activities, as well as proven knowledge and skills in accounting and finance, business judgment and strategy. A written definition of "independence" should also be incorporated into the qualification guidelines. The board of directors should make an annual determination regarding the independence of directors based on applicable criteria, such as the NYSE and Nasdaq rules, and prepare a report disclosing the basis for such determinations.

Financial Expertise

All companies with listed securities, even those whose securities are not traded on the NYSE or Nasdaq, must make specified disclosures regarding the financial expertise of the members of their audit committee. In addition, companies with securities listed on one of the main exchanges must ensure that their audit committee members are all able to satisfy basic "financial literacy" requirements, including the ability to read and understand financial statements. Realizing the practical and public relations advantages of recruiting board members that are well versed in financial reporting and accounting issues, companies are beginning to adopt policies with respect to director qualifications that emphasize the need to find candidates with education and experience as a public accountant, auditor, principal financial officer, controller or principal accounting officer of a company, or a position involving similar functions; experience actively supervising a principal financial officer, principal accounting officer, controller, public accountant, auditor or person performing similar functions; or experience overseeing or assessing the performance of companies or public accountants with respect to the preparation, auditing or evaluation of financial statements.

Charter and Activities of Governance and Nominating Committee

The NYSE requires that the responsibilities of the nominating/corporate governance committee must be explicitly spelled out in a committee charter and it is customary for the charter to be included in the company's proxy statement and posted on the company's website. The charter should state the purposes of the committee, as described above (i.e., recommending nominees for the board and developing corporate governance principles), and should describe the committee's goals and responsibilities, which must include, at a minimum, oversight of the evaluation of the board of directors and management, as well as a statement of the criterion that should be used for selection of directors.[7] Nasdaq-listed companies must certify that they have adopted a formal written charter for the nominations committee or board resolution, as applicable, addressing the nominations process and such related matters as may be required under the federal securities laws.[8] Other responsibilities of the committee that are typically part of the charter include reviewing candidate qualifications and potential conflicts of interest, assessment of the contributions of board members being considered for re-nomination, monitoring and safeguarding the independence of the board, and overseeing and reviewing the company's internal processes for communicating information to the board on a timely basis. The committee should also orchestrate director orientation and continuing education programs.[9]

Statement of Purpose

The traditional stated purpose of the governance and nominating committee, which remains central to its activities today, has been assisting

the board of directors in identifying, screening and recommending qualified candidates to serve as directors of the company, taking into account
applicable legal requirements, and in maintaining oversight of the board
of directors' operations and effectiveness. Going forward, however, it can
be expected that purpose statements will be updated to take into account
Global Compact recommendations that they include a statement about
ensuring the board fulfills its sustainability responsibilities in addition to
legal, ethical and functional responsibilities.[10]

Composition, Meetings and Procedures

The governance and nominating committee generally includes at least
two members of the board, each of whom must satisfy the independence
standards of the applicable listing requirements and otherwise be free from
any relationship that, in the judgment of the board, would interfere with his
or her exercise of business judgment as a committee member. Committee
meetings should be regularly scheduled during the course of the year with
the expectation that additional meetings may be required during times
when the committee is actively engaged in soliciting and vetting candidates
for board membership. In discharging its responsibilities, the committee
should have sole authority to, as it deems appropriate, select, retain and/
or replace, as needed, search firms used to identify director candidates and
other outside advisors, including advisors on director compensation, to
provide independent advice to the committee. The governance and nominating committee should have access to outside counsel with specific
expertise in governance issues in order to ensure that the company's corporate governance policies are up-to-date and provide assistance to the
committee in situations where it is called upon to remediate potential
conflict-of-interest transactions. The composition of the governance and
nominating committee should also reflect that board's aspirations with
regard to diversity.

Scope of Duties and Responsibilities

In general, the duties and responsibilities of the governance and nominating committee typically highlighted in committee charters include:

- Recommending to the board candidates for election or re-election
  to the board at each annual meeting of shareowners of the company
  including assessment of the contribution of board members being
  considered for re-election
- Recommending to the board candidates for election by the board to
  fill vacancies occurring on the board
- Considering shareowner nominees for board seats
- Monitoring the independence of the board

- Making recommendations to the board concerning the selection criteria to be used by the committee in seeking nominees for election to the board including procedures for review of candidate qualifications and potential conflicts of interest
- Aiding in attracting qualified candidates to serve on the board
- Making recommendations to the board concerning the structure, composition and functioning of the board and all board committees including the membership and scope of activities of specific committees
- Reviewing board meeting procedures, including the appropriateness, adequacy and timeliness of the information supplied to directors prior to and during board meetings
- Establishing policies and procedures for reviewing related-party transactions
- Evaluating or providing for evaluation of board and board committee performance and the performance of individual directors
- Reviewing and recommending retirement policies for directors
- Reviewing any outside directorships in other public companies held by senior company officials
- Periodically receiving and considering recommendations from the CEO regarding succession at the CEO and other senior officer levels
- Developing and recommending a set of corporate governance principles to the board
- Making reports and recommendations to the board within the scope of its functions

Governance and nominating committees have special duties and responsibilities with respect to governance, social and environmental responsibility matters that should be affirmatively reflected in the committee charter such as:

- Developing, recommending to the board and overseeing corporate governance principles and guidelines applicable to the board, management and the rest of the company
- Reviewing and assessing, no less frequently than annually, the appropriateness of the company's governance principles and practices and making recommendations to the board with respect to changes in those principles or practices
- Overseeing and making recommendations to the board concerning the company's code of business conduct and ethics and conflicts of interest policies as applicable to directors
- In concert with the board and the board-level CSR, reviewing and assessing company policies and practices with respect to significant issues of CSR and corporate sustainability
- Periodically reviewing and assessing the company's communication to shareholders and all other stakeholders with respect to its policies and

practices in the areas of corporate governance and CSR, including the communications contained on the company's website

A Global Compact publication recommended that the specific duties and responsibilities of the governance and nomination committee should also include the following:[11]

- Ensuring the board demonstrates best practice in corporate sustainability governance and effectiveness and that a periodic review is conducted to ensure board practices continue to align with best practices in corporate sustainability governance
- Developing, maintaining, evaluating and updating a corporate sustainability governance framework which describes the corporate sustainability governance processes in the organization
- Ensuring that processes for identifying, recruiting, appointing and providing ongoing development for directors reflect best corporate sustainability governance practices
- Assessing the effectiveness of the board nomination process at furthering the company's sustainability objectives
- Considering the board's operating practices and ensuring they adhere to best practices with respect to sustainability impacts (e.g. green meeting standards, travel, accommodations, etc.)
- Implementing and executing long-term board composition plans and nomination criteria that reference sustainability competencies, skills, strengths, experience, background and knowledge and reference the board's commitment and approach to sustainability and diversity
- Developing a skills matrix/competencies grid and criteria for board membership that includes sustainability, diversity and values alignment
- Ensuring that annual report/disclosure on governance practices describes the board's corporate sustainability governance practices in accordance with the Global Reporting Initiative guidelines or other recognized standard
- Facilitating the integration of sustainability into orientation of new directors and ongoing training and education for the overall board and individual directors and ensuring that the sustainability skills, experience and contribution of the overall board and individual directors is incorporated into the board's evaluation processes

Evaluations of board and management performance should be conducted no less frequently than annually by the governance and nominating committee and the committee should have the sole authority, supported by adequate funding, to retain and dismiss outside advisors that may provide consulting services in connection with the committee's responsibilities, such as search firms used to identify board and management candidates.

Identification and Selection of Qualified Directors

An effective board of directors should operate as a team and should be composed of members that, taken together, can contribute the requisite technical, operational, financial and managerial experience and talents to the deliberations of the board. The composition of the board of directors for a public company is dictated, to some extent, by the regulatory requirements and the listing standards of the national securities exchanges and this means that the director group for a public company must include independent directors and directors with appropriate credentials in specific areas such as accounting and financial reporting.

Recruitment and selection of new board members has traditionally been left either to the CEO or to a group of directors on a nominating committee who meet only during that period of the year when the bylaws require that directors be nominated and put before the shareholders for election. The preferred approach is for the board to take the time to adopt guidelines to be followed in order to establish and maintain an orderly process for recruiting and selecting new members for its board of directors. The center piece of those guidelines should be the establishment of a permanent committee that is committed to working year-round on board development including not only the traditional recruiting and selection activities but also mapping out a long-term strategy for the composition of the board and ensuring that current board members are informed about "best practices" for being knowledgeable and effective board members.

The board development committee should draft a comprehensive policy that covers the process of identifying, selecting and vetting potential nominees for the board; qualifications for selection, both personal and professional; procedures for handling shareholder nominations, which are particularly relevant for public companies subject to specific statutory requirements relating to such nominations; election and orientation; performance assessment and re-election.

In discharging its responsibilities with respect to identifying and recruiting new directors who can broaden the range of experience and expertise available to the full board and its committees, the nominating committee should pay specific attention to identifying candidates with experience in evaluating and overseeing CSR and corporate sustainability initiatives, such as CEOs of other companies that have achieved positive recognition for their sustainability efforts. The nominating committee can also contribute to the socially responsible profile of the company by ensuring that the board is diverse and represents all the company's key constituencies and that members have the skills and experience necessary to engage effectively with stakeholders regarding CSR and corporate sustainability and to identify and manage risks. The committee should integrate sustainability criteria into its processes for identifying director candidates and evaluating director performance.

Governance Codes and Policy Statements

One of the most important duties of the governance and nominating committee is the adoption and dissemination of appropriate corporate governance policies and procedures. Written policies and procedures are not only important in making sure that the corporate governance program is properly implemented and monitored; they can also serve as a useful public relations tool. Policies and procedures typically adopted by the board of directors include corporate governance guidelines; director qualifications and selection procedures and definition of independence; committee charters; code of ethics for senior financial officers; CEO and chief financial officer (CFO) certification of financial statements (through links to actual filings of periodic reports containing such certifications); procedures for selection of outside auditors and rotation of audit partners; description of compensation policies for senior executives; corporate code of conduct; methods for contacting company officials; and description of board, committee and officer evaluation processes. Each of the policies should be drafted by in-house and outside counsel, reviewed by the governance and nominating committee and any other board committees that may have oversight over the topics addressed in the policy, and ultimately approved by formal action of the entire board of directors. All of the policies should be distributed to employees, perhaps by posting on the company's intranet, and it is essential that the policies and related procedures be regularly reviewed at the company's employee training sessions.[12]

Directors' Education and Performance Assessment

Accepted notions of good corporate governance dictate the implementation of director education programs and regular assessments of the performance of the board of directors. In fact, the NYSE requires that the boards of its listed companies adopt and disclose corporate governance guidelines that address, among other things, continuing education and orientation of directors and annual performance evaluations of the board. Education is an imperative for board members confronting a continuous stream of new economic, environmental and social issues and a constantly shifting pool of compliance matters and risk management concerns. As for assessment, consultants such as EY have argued that assessment should go beyond simply confirming that the board members have the right skills and experience and be perceived as opportunities to provide clarity on the roles of directors and the board as a whole; accelerate decision making and avoid unnecessary director conflicts; strengthen understanding of business operations, customer experience and people management practices as the organization evolves; identify gaps in knowledge and expertise related to rapid changes in technology, including digital, cyber and other associated risks and opportunities for the company; and develop deeper understanding of the sector or industry dynamics and competitive threats.[13]

A Global Compact publication recommended that all board members should have generic sustainability skills and knowledge such as basic awareness of sustainability and how it affects the organization; basic understanding of what is corporate sustainability; ability to identify at a high level the most material sustainability impacts of and on the organization, its value chain, industry and operating context; knowledge of key stakeholders and their priorities and issues; understanding of how poor sustainability performance can create reputational and other risks; ability to articulate how sustainability relates to the purpose and strategy of the organization; understanding of sustainability trends generally and as they affect the industry and their impact on the company; and knowledge of the company's business case for sustainability, including how sustainability can contribute to long-term value creation such as the ability to attract and retain talent and stimulate innovation.[14] The committee should ensure that all directors are adequately versed in the sustainability-related topics of most interest to investors such as climate change and identifying and mitigating the risks associated with climate change. Education and training should also cover emerging trends in the sustainability area.

Evaluation of Board and Committee Performance

Boards of public companies must, as a matter of good practice and in accordance with specific legal and regulatory requirements, conduct regular evaluations of the performance of the board as a whole as well as each of the individual directors. NYSE-listed companies must include annual performance evaluations of the board in their corporate governance guidelines. In addition, the NYSE requires that its listed companies establish an independent nominating/governance committee that will be responsible for overseeing the evaluation of the board and management. Evaluation activities are not limited to the board of directors as a whole but must also be conducted with respect to activities of key board committees.

Board evaluation is a relatively new phenomenon and standards are still emerging on the right questions to ask and how assessments should be conducted. Moreover, in order for the evaluation and assessment to be meaningful there needs to be some understanding as to just what is meant by the term "effective board". One report on board evaluation advised that in order for the board to be effective it must have the right people, the right culture, the right issues, the right information, the right process and the right follow-through.[15] Each of these elements can be explained briefly as follows:

- The board should have a substantial majority of independent directors with a wide range of talents, expertise, and occupational and personal

backgrounds as well as an independent-minded spirit to act courageously for the best interests of the corporation and its shareholders
- The board should develop and encourage an internal culture that promotes candid communication and a rigorous approach to collecting and evaluating information and making difficult decisions regarding issues that are appropriate for the board
- The board should focus its attention and activities on the design, implementation and assessment of corporate strategy and should be actively involved, in conjunction with management, on all issues that are materially relevant to maximization of long-term shareholder value
- Directors must have access to, and carefully review, all relevant information necessary for them to make informed decisions; however, when requesting information directors must make reasonable demands that allow management to provide prompt and thorough replies
- The board should establish a formal evaluation process that begins with developing a description of the specific duties, goals and objectives of the board as a whole and each of the directors individually, and then deploying the tools necessary to measure actual performance against those responsibilities
- Once the evaluation is completed the results should be shared with the full board as well as each individual director and action plans should be developed in order to address areas in which improvement is necessary

Boards of public companies typically delegate the evaluation and assessment process to an independent committee, generally the nominating/governance committee. The members of that committee should be versed in the methods and tools that have been developed to make the assessment process more efficient and objective including the use of questionnaires and interviews.[16] Individual evaluation of directors can be carried out in a variety of ways including self-evaluation, peer evaluation, a combination of self-evaluation and peer evaluation, evaluation by the nominating/governance committee and evaluation by an outside consultant. Hopefully one of the byproducts of the evaluation and assessment process is that the directors gain a fuller appreciation of their value to the company and the important role that they can play in setting and executing company strategy and supporting the activities of the management team that they are overseeing. The results of the evaluation should be taken seriously and the board should formally accept recommendations for improvement and require progress reports on remedial actions as a regular part of the board agenda.[17]

Like all other board-level committees, the governance and nominating committee should conduct an annual evaluation of its performance and effectiveness, which may be a self-evaluation or an evaluation employing such other resources or procedures as the committee may deem appropriate.

The committee should also review and reassess its charter on a periodic basis and submit any recommended changes to the board for its consideration. In addition, as discussed above, the governance and nominating committee is responsible for the annual performance reviews for the entire board of directors and each of the individual members of the board. EY suggested that the governance and nominating committee should consider the following questions in the course of performing its own performance assessment:[18]

- Is the board's skills matrix aligned to the company's going-forward strategy? Is this process dynamic and formalized?
- How is the committee ensuring that the educational needs of its directors are being met given ongoing industry disruption and convergence, which are resulting in changes to the company's strategy and risk management?
- Is the committee structure still appropriate given the ever-expanding board agenda?
- Is "diversity" formally defined as including considerations such as age, gender, geography, skills, race or ethnicity?
- Does the board have a stakeholder engagement and communication policy? If so, is the policy and related responsibilities formalized in the company's governance documents?

Notes

1 See generally NYSE Listing Manual § 303A.04.
2 See generally Nasdaq Rule 5605(e) and Nasdaq Listing Rule IM-5605-7.
3 *ESG, Strategy and the Long View: A Framework for Board Oversight* (KPMG LLP, 2017), 6.
4 See generally NYSE Listing Manual § 303A.01, 303A.03 and Nasdaq Rule 5605(b).
5 See NYSE Listing Manual § 303A.05.
6 Nasdaq Rule 5605(d).
7 NYSE Listing Manual § 303A.04(b). The Commentary to NYSE Listing Manual § 303A.04(b) suggests that the nominating/corporate governance committee charter should also address the following items: committee member qualifications; committee member appointment and removal; committee structure and operations (including authority to delegate to subcommittees); and committee reporting to the board.
8 Nasdaq Rule 5605(e)(2).
9 For examples of governance and nominating committee charters and additional commentary on preparation of such charters, see "Board Committee Charters" in the management tools available as part of "Governance: A Library of Resources for Sustainable Entrepreneurs" prepared and distributed by the Sustainable Entrepreneurship Project available at (www.seproject.org).

10 *The Essential Role of the Corporate Secretary to Enhance Board Sustainability Oversight: A Best Practices Guide* (United Nations Global Compact, September 2016).

11 Id.

12 For further discussion of corporate governance policies and procedures, see Chapter 11 (Internal Governance Instruments) in this volume.

13 EY Center for Board Matters, *Accelerating Board Performance: The Importance of Assessments*, available at www.ey.com/Publication/vwLUAssets/ey-accelerating-board-performance-through-assessments/$File/ey-accelerating-board-performance-through-assessments.pdf (accessed May 13, 2020).

14 *The Essential Role of the Corporate Secretary to Enhance Board Sustainability Oversight: A Best Practices Guide* (United Nations Global Compact, September 2016).

15 See *Report of the NACD Blue Ribbon Commission on Board Evaluation: Improving Director Effectiveness* (2001/2005).

16 Id. (includes examples of sample forms that can be used for board evaluation and the evaluation of individual directors).

17 For further information on performing a board assessment, including elements of board effectiveness, explanations of approaches to evaluation and a sample board evaluation with annotated discussion questions, see EY Center for Board Matters, *Accelerating Board Performance: The Importance of Assessments*, available at www.ey.com/Publication/vwLUAssets/ey-accelerating-board-performance-through-assessments/$File/ey-accelerating-board-performance-through-assessments.pdf (accessed May 13, 2020).

18 EY Center for Board Matters, A Look Inside Nominating and Governance Committees, available at www.ey.com/us/en/issues/governance-and-reporting/ey-a-look-inside-nominating-and-governance-committees

5   Audit Committee

In the wake of the criticisms of auditors and their corporate oversees for their failures during the financial debacles of the late 1990s and early 2000s, board-level audit committees of public companies became the foundation of many aspects of a new corporate governance scheme and emerged as the most important of the board committees. Under pressure from investors and consumers, Congress passed, and the President signed, the Sarbanes-Oxley Act of 2002 (SOX) which, among other things, included Section 301 amending Section 10A of the Exchange Act of 1934, as amended (Exchange Act),[1] to require that the SEC promulgate rules directing the national securities exchanges and national securities associations to prohibit the listing of any security of an issuer that is not in compliance with any portion of the following requirements relating to audit committees of the issuer:

- The audit committee of each issuer, in its capacity as a committee of the board of directors, must be directly responsible for the appointment, compensation, and oversight of the work of any registered public accounting firm employed by that issuer (including resolution of disagreements between management and the auditor regarding financial reporting) for the purpose of preparing or issuing an audit report or related work, and each such registered public accounting firm must report directly to the audit committee.[2]
- Each member of the audit committee of the issuer must be a member of the board of directors of the issuer, and shall otherwise be independent. In order to be considered to be independent for purposes of this requirement, a member of an audit committee of an issuer may not, other than in his or her capacity as a member of the audit committee, the board of directors, or any other board committee (i) accept any consulting, advisory, or other compensatory fee from the issuer; or (ii) be an affiliated person of the issuer or any subsidiary thereof.[3]
- Each audit committee shall establish procedures for (A) the receipt, retention, and treatment of complaints received by the issuer regarding accounting, internal accounting controls, or auditing matters; and

(B) the confidential, anonymous submission by employees of the issuer of concerns regarding questionable accounting or auditing matters.[4]

- Each audit committee must have the authority to engage independent counsel and other advisers, as it determines necessary to carry out its duties.[5]
- Each issuer must provide for appropriate funding, as determined by the audit committee, in its capacity as a committee of the board of directors, for payment of compensation (A) to the registered public accounting firm employed by the issuer for the purpose of rendering or issuing an audit report; and (B) to any advisers employed by the audit committee as contemplated above.[6]

The SEC subsequently adopted rules (Exchange Act Rule 10A-3) putting SOX § 301 into effect and both national securities exchanges adopted listing standards regarding the independence of audit committee members of listed companies and a wide array of other matters consistent with the requirements of SOX § 301 and the SEC rules.[7] For example, there are now specific rules regarding the structure and composition of audit committees, and such committees have now been given broad responsibilities with respect to oversight of various activities and procedures include engagement of outside auditing firms, establishment and monitoring of internal controls and creation of procedures for receipt and investigation of complaints regarding questionable accounting or auditing matters. The audit committee is also a key participant in the company's efforts to assess risks and develop and implement risk management strategies. Minimum qualifications for service on an audit committee have been promulgated by the SEC and the major exchanges and place a premium on independence, education and experience in the accounting and finance areas and the ability to critically evaluate the recommendations and decisions of senior management and the independent auditors with respect to financial reporting issues. In light of the importance of the audit committee, it is not surprising that SEC rules expanded the disclosure requirements regarding the makeup and activities of audit committees.

Charter and Activities of Audit Committee

Given the enormous responsibilities of the audit committee and its members, close attention should be given to establishing and maintaining appropriate procedures relating to committee activities. First and foremost, the audit committee, as well as the entire board of directors, should draft and adopt a written audit committee charter that specifies the main purposes of the committee, the duties and responsibilities of the committee, and the structure, processes and membership requirements associated with the committee.[8] When drafting the charter, which should appear in the company's proxy materials and be posted on the company's website, it is important to consider the specific requirements of SOX and any relevant listing requirements applicable to the company. In that regard, both the NYSE and Nasdaq have adopted requirements mandating that audit committees have a written charter that covers the matters set out in the applicable listing standards.[9]

Statement of Purpose

The primary purpose of the audit committee is oversight of the integrity of the company's financial statements; however, additional issues typically included in the statement of purpose include oversight of the company's risk management and internal control arrangements; oversight of compliance with legal and regulatory requirements; making recommendations to the entire board of directors regarding the selection of the company's independent auditors and the compensation payable to the auditors; oversight of the performance, qualifications and independence of the company's independent accountants; promulgation and enforcement of policies and procedures relating to the work performed by the independent auditors; and oversight of the performance of the company's internal audit function. A Global Compact publication recommended that the purpose statement of the audit committee charter also include ensuring the integrity of the company's sustainability performance statements and sustainability information communicated externally and conducting oversight of compliance with the company's sustainability policy or commitments (e.g., via an internal audit review).[10] The potential scope of the areas of concern for the audit committee is obviously quite large and may be reduced significantly in situations where the board has created separate board-level committees to oversee issues relating to compliance and risk management, disclosure and reporting and CSR; however, even when such committees have been created it will be necessary for the audit committee to collaborate closely with them in areas related to the content and integrity of the company's financial statements.

Composition, Meetings and Procedures

The SEC, as well the various exchanges, has adopted rules and regulations relating to the composition of audit committees, as well as the specific skills and background of members of such committees. Under SOX, every member of the audit committee must be independent, with "independence" determined by reference to detailed definitions promulgated by the SEC and the exchanges. Most public companies have provided that a majority of their audit committee members be independent for a number of years and the NYSE and Nasdaq have both historically required that all listed companies must have an audit committee, composed of at least three members, all of whom must be independent (subject to limited exceptions under Nasdaq rules). However, the hurdle for establishing independence was never as high as it became after the adoption of SOX. The overriding objective is to ensure that audit committee members are no longer beholden to senior management and that they are comfortable exercising authority that, in a number of cases, may result in decisions that are at variance with the wishes of management.

Another interesting development has been the promulgation of functional qualifications for service as a member of the audit committee. Companies must disclose in their annual and quarterly reports whether or not the audit committee includes at least one member who is a "financial expert" (and, if not, the reasons for the lack of such an expert), subject to certain exceptions. This requirement applies not only to "listed companies", but to all companies whose securities trade in the United States (even if none of the company's securities are listed on a national exchange).[11] SEC rules define an "audit committee financial expert" as a person who has all the following attributes:[12]

- An understanding of generally accepted accounting principles (GAAP) and financial statements;
- The ability to assess the general application of GAAP in connection with the accounting for estimates, accruals, and reserves;
- Experience in preparing, auditing, analyzing, or evaluating financial statements that present a breadth and level of complexity of accounting issues that are generally comparable to the breadth and complexity of issues that can reasonably be expected to be raised by a company's financial statements, or experience actively supervising one or more persons engaged in such activities;
- An understanding of internal controls and procedures for financial reporting; and
- An understanding of audit committee functions.

The SEC rules mention the following alternative means for a person to have acquired the necessary attributes listed above:[13]

- Education and experience as a principal financial officer, principal accounting officer, controller, public accountant, or auditor or experience in one or more positions that involve the performance of similar functions;
- Experience actively supervising a principal financial officer, principal accounting officer, controller, public accountant, auditor, or person performing similar functions;
- Experience overseeing or assessing the performance of companies or public accountants with respect to the preparation, auditing, or evaluation of financial statements; or
- Other relevant experience.

Both the NYSE and Nasdaq also have "financial literacy" requirements that must be satisfied by each member of the audit committee of a listed company.[14] As a result, audit committee members must come prepared to understand the complex rules that generally apply to preparation of financial statements and determination of accounting policies. This can be a challenge even to the most experienced directors, including those that have a background in the accounting field, since requirements and practices are changing rapidly on a regular basis. Companies should initiate training and educational programs for their directors or, at a minimum, require that audit committee members attend and complete similar programs conducted by the NYSE or Nasdaq.

Members of the audit committee must be prepared to spend a substantial amount of time in discharging their duties and obligations in relation to the company. For example, commentators are advising that audit committees should schedule full-day meetings on no less than a quarterly basis. The schedule for the meetings should allow sufficient time to review earnings releases and proposed 10-Q filings. The chairperson of the audit committee plays a key role in ensuring that the time of the committee members is invested wisely and efficiently and he or she needs to be prepared to work on the committee agenda to make sure that meetings run smoothly and coordinate with other committees, such as the compliance and risk management committee and the disclosure and reporting committee, to avoid unnecessary waste of effort through duplication. The committee chairperson should also have a good understanding of the business and its risks and controls; be professionally skeptical and possess integrity and confidence; have strong communication and interpersonal skills; and be prepared and willing to set aside a large amount of time to overseeing the committee's agenda and projects and meeting with management, other board members, the independent auditors, members of the internal audit function and representatives of key stakeholders.[15]

Given the time required by audit committee members to complete the necessary consultations, it is more important than ever that audit committee meetings and activities be carefully scheduled. This requires proper advance planning for meetings, including timely dissemination of the materials to be discussed at the meeting, and sufficient time during the meetings to accomplish all the work that needs to be done. In addition, audit committee members must anticipate the need to devote additional time for follow-up on questions and issues that arise at the meetings. All of this means that each prospective audit committee member should evaluate carefully the existing demands on his or her time before accepting this important assignment and the Commentary to the NYSE listing standards actually includes conditions that must be satisfied before an audit committee member will be allowed to simultaneously serve on the audit committees of more than three public companies.[16] Audit committee members should also expect to be tapped for assignment to other board-level committees that handle topics that overlap with the traditional responsibilities of the audit committee in order to ensure that there is effective coordination and collaboration between those committees. For example, audit committee members are good candidates for service on the board's compliance and risk management and disclosure and reporting committees.

Given the broad array of duties and responsibilities that have been vested with the audit committee, and the corresponding need for interpretation of applicable rules and regulations, it is not surprising to find that the audit committee will often require focused advice from independent counsel. Recognizing this need, SEC rules now provide the audit committee with authority, as discussed above, to engage independent counsel and any other advisors the committee determines may be necessary in order for it to carry out its duties and obligations. For example, it can be expected that counsel will be consulted for interpretation of basic issues, such as whether a nominee for the audit committee is "independent" or whether a particular service provided by an accounting firm falls within the scope of the audit committee's approval requirements. Counsel will also be required to assist the audit committee in the development of rules and procedures, including written charters that must be developed to define the scope of audit committee activities. Finally, counsel will be required to assist the committee in overseeing and conducting internal investigations that may be brought to the attention of the committee through the professional standards requirements imposed on attorneys.

Scope of Duties and Responsibilities

As a general rule, regardless of the relevant listing requirements, the charter should cover each of the key activities and duties of the audit committee, including supervision of the company's relationship with its independent auditor, covering such matters as selection, evaluation, and auditor staffing; development of policies regarding non-audit services; review and discussion of the company's financial statements and critical accounting policies with management and the independent auditor; review of all related-party transactions; oversight of the company's internal controls; development of policies for hiring former auditor personnel; and development of policies regarding the declaration of dividends and other distributions to shareholders.

Nasdaq Listing Rule 5605(c)(3) requires that the audit committee must have the specific audit committee responsibilities and authority necessary to comply with Rule 10A-3(b)(2), (3), (4) and (5) under the Exchange Act (subject to the exemptions provided in Rule 10A-3(c) under the Exchange Act), concerning responsibilities relating to: (i) registered public accounting firms, (ii) complaints relating to accounting, internal accounting controls or auditing matters, (iii) authority to engage advisors and (iv) funding as determined by the audit committee. The NYSE requires that the charters of audit committees describe the details of a long list of audit committee duties and responsibilities including:[17]

- Retaining and terminating the independent auditors of the company;
- At least annually, obtaining and reviewing a report by the independent auditor relating to the auditor's internal control procedures and all relationships between the auditor and the company;
- Discussing the annual audited financial statement and quarterly financial statements with management and the independent auditor and the company's disclosure in the related "Management's Discussion and Analysis of Financial Condition and Results of Operations";
- Discussing earnings press releases, as well as financial information and earnings guidance given to analysts and rating agencies;
- Obtaining the advice and assistance of outside legal, accounting or other advisors, as appropriate;
- Discussing policies with respect to risk assessment and risk management;
- Meeting separately, periodically, with management, with the internal auditors, and with the independent auditors;
- Reviewing with the independent auditor any audit problems or difficulties and management's response;
- Setting clear hiring policies for employees or former employees of the independent auditor;
- Reporting regularly to the board on any issues that arise within its oversight responsibilities including the quality and integrity of the company's financial statements, the company's compliance with legal or regulatory requirements, the performance and independence of the auditors and the performance of the company's internal audit function;
- Preparing the report of the audit committee that SEC rules require to be included in the company's annual proxy statement; and
- Conducting an annual evaluation of its performance of its responsibilities.

Oversight of the Integrity of the Company's Financial Statements

The audit committee is the primary group within the board of directors with respect to overseeing the integrity of the company's financial statements and most of the committee's duties and responsibilities will be focused on ensuring that all material information regarding the company's financial and business performance is collected, analyzed and presented in a manner that satisfies not only regulatory requirements and industry standards but also fulfills the needs and expectations of each of the company's stakeholder groups. Specific activities to be performed by the committee with respect to the integrity of the financial statements include regularly reviewing the company's internal and external financial reporting systems; reviewing significant accounting and reporting issues and how these issues are being addressed including any significant changes in accounting principles and the methods used to account for significant or unusual transactions where different approaches are possible; reporting to the entire board of directors when the committee is not satisfied with any aspect of the company's proposed financial reporting; reviewing any material off-balance sheet transactions, arrangements, obligations and other relationships with unconsolidated entities or other persons that may have a material effect on the company and its related entities; reviewing and approving the publication of the company's quarterly and annual financial statements and related reports regarding the overall business of the company (including clarity and completeness of disclosure) to ensure that, taken as a whole, they are fair, balanced and understandable; reviewing the company's practices with regard to the release and publication of financial and other business information to the markets; and overseeing the assurance of the financial and non-financial key performance indicators in the company's financial and sustainability reports.

Relationships with Auditors

Historically, the selection of the independent auditor for a public company was managed by senior management, generally with little input from the audit committee or other outside directors. As a result, concerns arose, often legitimately, that independent auditors might be beholden to senior management and would be subject to undue influence with respect to determination of accounting policies and reporting of financial results. It is not surprising, therefore, that one of the most important changes implemented in SOX was to provide that the audit committee (composed entirely of independent directors as described above) must have authority over, and be made "directly responsible" for, appointing, compensating and retaining the company's independent auditor and for overseeing the work of the auditor in connection with the preparation or issuance of any audit report.[18] Among other things, this authority includes the right to determine the funds to be allocated to compensate the independent auditors for audit work and any related work, as well as the funds needed for other audit, review or attest services provided by a public accounting firm. In addition, these duties include the resolution of any disagreements between the auditor and company management relating to financial reporting. The rules and regulations also require that the audit committee (or the full board of directors) must approve all audit services (including delivery of a comfort letter in connection with an offering of securities) and, subject to certain de minimis exceptions, all permitted non-audit services to be provided by the auditor or its associated persons before the services are provided.[19]

Disclosure Controls, Compliance and Risk Management

SOX vested several significant compliance responsibilities in the audit committee. Perhaps most importantly, the audit committee was given a central role with respect to review of the company's disclosure documents and ensuring that all the financial and other information included therein has been properly prepared. Many companies retain oversight responsibility for disclosures and disclosure controls with the audit committee; however, in this publication it is assumed that the board creates a separate disclosure and reporting committee, often staffed with directors who are also serving as members of the audit committee.[20] In order to fulfill these tasks, audit committee and disclosure and reporting committee members must have a keen understanding of the company's internal controls, as well as the current state of the art with respect to financial accounting principles. The responsible committee must consult regularly with the company's independent auditors and senior managers, and should also meet with heads of various business units to verify that the company's control systems are being used throughout the organization. While emphasis should certainly be placed on the company's periodic reports, the procedures should be broad enough to include earnings releases and earnings guidance that is supplied to analysts and rating agencies. In addition, unless the board has created a separate compliance and risk management committee, the audit committee must assume various responsibilities relating to the company's compliance program including establishing codes and policies with respect to legal and regulatory compliance, risk assessment and risk management.[21]

Approval of Related-Party and Conflict-of-Interest Transactions

Nasdaq rules require that any "related-party transaction" be approved by the audit committee (or a comparable independent body of the board) as part of the company's obligation to conduct an appropriate review on an ongoing basis of such transactions. For purposes of these rules, a "related-party transaction" refers to a transaction that would have to be disclosed under Item 404 of SEC Regulation S-K.[22] No specific provisions on this subject are currently included in the NYSE rules; however, it is common for audit committees of NYSE-listed companies to take on oversight responsibility for such transactions in their written charters. As part of this authority, the audit committee must oversee compliance with § 402 of SOX, which provides that no public company may make, extend, modify or renew any personal loan to its executive officers or directors except for loans made in the ordinary course of the company's business, on market terms, for home improvement and manufactured home loans and for consumer credit, or extension of credit under an open-end credit plan or charge card.[23]

Internal Audit Function

The NYSE listing rules require that each listed company must have an internal audit function that is subject to the overall oversight responsibility of the audit committee.[24] The internal audit function must provide management and the audit committee with ongoing assessments of the company's risk management processes and system of internal control. A company may choose to outsource this function to a third party service provider other than its independent auditor.[25] The audit committee should expect to regularly receive and review status reports from the head of the internal audit function on controls and actions taken to resolve the issues raised; review the internal audit function including development of a charter and scope of duties and responsibilities, annual plan and associated timetable and budget and resource requirements; review the effectiveness of the internal audit function (including management's responsiveness to internal audit's findings and recommendations); approve the appointment and removal of the head of the internal audit function and meet with the head of the internal audit function at least annually without management.

Sustainability

The audit committee, working in collaboration with the board's CSR committee, should be expected to play an important role in overseeing the company's sustainability policy, commitments, procedures and reporting.[26] Some of the specific duties and responsibilities of the committee in this area include:[27]

- Monitoring compliance with sustainability policy, commitments and regulations; ensuring internal audit procedures are in place to assess cross-company compliance with sustainability commitments, policies and management systems; reviewing results of internal audits of compliance with sustainability policies, commitments and regulations
- Reviewing integrity of the organization's sustainability information systems and reporting processes, both internal and external; ensuring the company has implemented adequate systems, controls and processes to support the compilation of key sustainability performance metrics appropriate for reliably tracking performance, setting targets, benchmarking, compensating executives and external reporting
- Ensuring sustainability information is consistent across corporate websites, social media and voluntary reports and that provided in government filings, financial statements, investor presentations and other corporate disclosures
- Ensuring a process is in place for timely, accurate, consistent and complete external sustainability reporting

- Monitoring developments, trends and best practices in sustainability accounting and reporting
- Ensuring sustainability is sufficiently addressed in the annual budget and business plan
- Ensuring tax policies and planning are fair and equitable and do not attract reputational risk
- Ensuring public policy positions of the company and the trade associations of which it is a member are consistent with the company's sustainability commitments
- Monitoring research and development on sustainability and ensuring compliance with new regulations and non-binding standards on sustainability along with other committees formed to focus specifically on compliance activities[28]

Audit Committee Reporting and Self-Assessment Requirements

In addition to its own meetings and deliberations, the audit committee should be prepared to present regular reports to the board of directors on the scope and performance of the committee's oversight responsibilities. In addition, the committee must prepare any reports that SEC rules may require to be included in the company's annual proxy statement or other filings. For example, companies must include in each annual proxy statement a report from the audit committee that contains the following information: whether the audit committee reviewed and discussed the audited financial statements with management; whether they discussed the matters required to be discussed under the Financial Accounting Standards Board's Statement on Auditing Standards No. 61; and whether they received from the auditors disclosures about auditor independence required by Independence Standards Board Statement No. 1 and discussed independence with the auditors. The report also has to say whether the audit committee recommended including the audited financial statements in the company's public reporting documents, whether the audit committee has a charter (the company must publish it at least once every three years) and must disclose the independence of the members of the audit committee (as judged by the listing standards to which the company is subject).

The audit committee should conduct an annual evaluation of its performance of its responsibilities, including an assessment of the sufficiency of its written charter. The assessment process should include internal evaluation of performance by the audit committee members themselves as well as collection of information from others that deal with the audit committee on a regular basis. Among other things, the audit committee should specifically measure the impact that it has had on the company as a whole and on the financial reporting process specifically. The relationship between the audit committee and the independent auditors should be measured as should the quality of communications between the committee and the CEO, CFO and other members of the management team. Sophisticated tools are now available to monitor the efficacy of internal controls and information derived from these tools should be used in assessing audit committee performance and identifying and implementing changes that should be made in the control environment. The assessment process is also an opportunity to make changes in the staffing of the committee and members should be asked to provide feedback on their own performance as well as their perception of the contributions made by other members of the committee.

Notes

1 15 USC § 78f
2 15 USC § 7240(2)
3 15 USC § 7240(3)
4 15 USC § 7240(4)
5 15 USC § 7240(5)
6 15 USC § 7240(6)
7 See NYSE Listing Manual §§ 303A.02–303A.07 (the Commentary to NYSE Listing Manual § 303A.06 provides that the Exchange will apply the requirements of Rule 10A-3 in a manner consistent with the guidance provided by the SEC in SEC Release No. 34-47654 (April 1, 2003)); Nasdaq Listing Rule IM-5605-5.
8 For examples of audit committee charters and additional commentary on preparation of such charters, see "Board Committee Charters" in the management tools available as part of "Governance: A Library of Resources for Sustainable Entrepreneurs" prepared and distributed by the Sustainable Entrepreneurship Project, available at (www.seproject.org).
9 See generally NYSE Listing Manual § 303A.07 and NASDAQ Rule 5605(c)(1).
10 *The Essential Role of the Corporate Secretary to Enhance Board Sustainability Oversight: A Best Practices Guide* (United Nations Global Compact, September 2016).
11 Sarbanes-Oxley Act § 407(a), 15 USC § 7265, and SEC Release No. 33–8177, Disclosure Required by Sections 406 and 407 of the Sarbanes-Oxley Act of 2002 (January 23, 2003).
12 See 15 USC § 7265(b); 17 CFR § 229.407(d)(5)(ii).
13 17 CFR § 229.407(d)(5)(iii).
14 See NYSE Listing Manual § 303A.07 and Nasdaq Rule 5605(c)(2).
15 See P. Loop, *What to Look for in an Effective Audit Committee Chair* (National Association of Corporate Directors, March 13, 2018), available at https://blog.nacdonline.org/2018/03/what-to-look-for-audit-chair/ (accessed May 13, 2020).
16 Commentary to NYSE Listing Manual § 303A.07.
17 NYSE Listing Manual § 303A.07(c)(iii).
18 See generally SEC Rule 10A-3, 17 CFR § 240.10A-3; NYSE Listing Manual § 303A.06 and 303A.07 and Nasdaq Rule 5605(c)(3).
19 Sarbanes-Oxley Act §§ 201 and 202 and Exchange Act Rules 10A(h) and (i).

20 For further discussion, see Chapter 10 (Disclosure and Reporting Committee) in this volume.

21 For further discussion, see Chapter 9 (Compliance and Risk Management Committee) in this volume.

22 See generally Nasdaq Rule 5630(a). A body will be considered to be "comparable" to the audit committee if all the directors that are members of such body are both "independent" under NASDAQ rules and disinterested in the transaction.

23 Sarbanes-Oxley Act § 402(a), 15 USC § 78m(k).

24 See generally NYSE Listing Manual § 303A.06 and 303A.07.

25 Commentary to NYSE Listing Manual § 303A.07(d).

26 For discussion of the duties and responsibilities of the board-level corporate social responsibility committee, see Chapter 7 (Corporate Social Responsibility Committee) in this volume.

27 *The Essential Role of the Corporate Secretary to Enhance Board Sustainability Oversight: A Best Practices Guide* (United Nations Global Compact, September 2016).

28 R. Sainty, "Engaging Boards of Directors at the Interface of Corporate Sustainability and Corporate Governance", *Governance Directions* (March 2016), 85, 87.

6 Compensation and Organizational Development Committee

The NYSE and the Nasdaq have each imposed requirements on their listed companies with respect to how they are expected to determine executive officers' compensation and have promulgated various rules relating to the establishment and composition of compensation committees, the purposes of such committees and procedures that they are expected to follow in discharging their duties.[1] As a general matter, compensation and organizational development committees are charged with reviewing and recommending the compensation philosophy and policies of the company, reviewing the employment arrangements with the CEO and setting the compensation for the CEO and either recommending or setting the compensation of other members of the senior management team. In addition, the committee should have oversight responsibility for the overall compensation structure and bonus policies of the company, with a particular focus on whether or not it creates appropriate incentives, including stock option and purchase plans, for managers and employees at all levels of the organization. Compensation packages for senior executives should be carefully scrutinized, and perhaps be made subject to review by the audit committee of the board of directors and approval by a vote of the shareholders.

The compensation committee should also carefully review the compensation and incentive programs, and accompanying evaluation procedures, established for the company's senior executives to ensure that they are consistent with the company's CSR and corporate sustainability initiatives and performance targets. Executive compensation has often been criticized as being tied too closely to short-term performance and weighting financial performance too heavily will dissuade executives from investing in sustainability initiatives that may be more difficult to objectively assess for value (e.g., improving energy efficiency, reducing greenhouse gas emissions, meeting health and safety targets, or improving leadership diversity).[2] The compensation committee should be proactively engaged in dialogue with the company's investors regarding sustainability and executive compensation.[3] The committee should also oversee the company's human resources development programs to ensure that they include CSR and corporate sustainability topics.

Compensation committees must provide and certify a report on executive compensation for each year's proxy statement and are also responsible for oversight of retirement and benefit plans; various organizational development issues including succession planning, organizational structure and leadership development; and retention of compensation advisors (including assessment of the independence of such advisors). As is the case with the audit and other board-level committees, compensation committees should expect to conduct an annual evaluation of their performance.

Charter and Activities of Compensation Committee

Both the NYSE and the Nasdaq require that the responsibilities of the compensation committee be explicitly spelled out in a written charter that should be included in the company's proxy statement and posted on the company's website.[4] While the specific requirements for the content of the charter will vary depending on which of the securities exchanges has oversight responsibilities for the company, the charter should include provisions, either voluntarily or in response to specific listing requirements, relating to the scope of the committee's responsibilities and how it carries out those responsibilities, including structure, processes and membership requirements; compliance with specific exchange requirements regarding the independence of committee members; and prohibitions on the CEO being present during voting or deliberations by the committee on his or her compensation. The charter should also specify that the committee will have sole authority to retain and terminate any compensation advisors to assist in the evaluation of director or senior executive compensation, including sole authority to approve the reasonable compensation and other terms of retention with respect to such advisors, should clearly acknowledge the company's obligations with respect to providing funding for the retention of any such advisor and should describe the committee's responsibilities with respect to considering specific independence factors before selecting advisors other than in-house legal counsel. Finally, the charter should include a requirement that the committee review and reassess the adequacy of the charter on an annual basis.

Statement of Purpose

The statement of purpose in the charter of the compensation and organizational development committee typically tracks the more specific duties and responsibilities for the committee included elsewhere in the charter and discussed in detail below. As a general matter, the purpose of the committee is to provide guidance to the entire board of directors, as well as to the members of the senior executive team of the company, with respect to their fiduciary and legal obligations pertaining to the compensation of the

CEO and certain other executive officers, as well as such other employees who are members of the company's senior management as the committee shall determine from time to time; the organizational structure of senior management; the succession, retention and training of senior management; the company's overall succession, retention and training programs; supervision of the company's overall compensation and benefits programs, including approval and oversight of grants pursuant to the company's equity compensation plans; the oversight of the company's retirement and employee health and welfare plans; and the oversight of the company's benefits programs and such other matters that directly impact the success and wellbeing of the company's human resources. A Global Compact publication recommended that the purpose statement of the compensation committee include motivating and rewarding sustainability performance in the executive compensation plan.[5] As a general matter, the compensation and organizational development committee focused on approving material compensation and benefit matters as well as setting high-level policy and strategy, and management remains responsible for the day-to-day administration of the human resources function.

Composition, Meetings and Procedures

"Independence" is the focal point of the requirements for membership on the compensation and organizational development committee. NYSE-listed companies must have a compensation committee composed entirely of independent directors and the entire board of directors is required to make an affirmative determination that each compensation committee member is independent under the general board independence standards set forth in the NYSE Listed Company Manual.[6] The Nasdaq listing rules provide that compensation of the CEO must be determined, or recommended to the board for determination, either by: (A) independent directors constituting a majority of the board's independent directors in a vote in which only independent directors participate; or (B) a compensation committee comprised solely of independent directors. The CEO may not be present during voting or deliberations.[7] Compensation of all other executive officers (defined as those officers covered in Rule 16a-1(f) under the Exchange Act[8]) must be determined, or recommended to the board for determination, either by: (A) independent directors constituting a majority of the board's independent directors in a vote in which only independent directors participate; or (B) a compensation committee comprised solely of independent directors.[9] A non-independent director may serve as a member of the compensation committee under exceptional and limited circumstances.[10]

As is the case with the audit committee, the compensation and organizational development committee maintains a busy schedule with a full agenda that extends throughout the company's fiscal year. As such, provision should be made for four to six regular meetings of the committee annually, generally corresponding with the schedule for meetings of the entire board of directors. Committee members should set aside time for meetings with the CEO to discuss compensation matters for other executive officers and organizational development issues. When appropriate, meetings should be held with administrators of the company's stock and other benefit plans and with compensation advisors that the committee may engage through the processes described above. The executive head of the company's human resources function is typically in attendance for most of the committee's meetings and is often responsible for the preparation of minutes of meetings and drafts of reports that the committee may deliver to the entire board.

Scope of Duties and Responsibilities

A comprehensive list of the duties and responsibilities of a compensation and organizational development committee would likely include obligations and authority to:

- Review the company's executive compensation programs to ensure the attraction, retention and appropriate reward of executive officers, to motivate their performance in the achievement of the company's business objectives, and to align the interest of executive officers with the long-term interests of the stockholders and other stakeholders of the company
- Review the company's executive compensation programs to ensure that they motivate executives and employees to engage in activities that will improve the company's sustainability performance and reward them for contributing to the success of such activities
- Review and approve corporate goals and objectives relevant to the annual compensation of the CEO, evaluate the CEO's performance in relation to such goals and objectives and, based on such evaluation, recommend to the independent directors for their approval, the CEO's annual compensation, including salary, bonus and equity and non-equity incentive compensation
- Review and approve, for the company's executive officers other than the CEO, annual compensation for such officers, including salary, bonus and equity and non-equity incentive compensation, based on recommendations from the CEO
- Review the company's equity and non-equity incentive compensation and other plans and recommend changes in such plans to the entire board of directors as needed, and act as the administrator of such plans on behalf of the board
- Review and approve grants and awards, and the terms and conditions thereof, under the company's equity incentive-based plans and review

and approve the terms of, and awards under, other incentive compensation plans that the company establishes for, or makes available to, the company's officers and other employees (including recommending to the independent directors for their approval such grants and awards to be made to the CEO)

- Review and set performance goals, as applicable, under the company's equity and non-equity incentive compensation plans
- Review and evaluate the pension, 401(k) and other benefit plans established by the company for officers and other employees and approve recommendations of management regarding such plans
- Serve as a resource to the CEO in matters relating to senior management selection, succession planning, management development and talent utilization, and report to the board or resources on progress on the company's organizational development activities including senior management selection, succession planning and training of all management levels
- Review and recommend to the board executive compensation and organizational development policies and processes
- Ensure that a report on executive compensation is prepared for inclusion in the company's annual proxy statement in accordance with applicable SEC rules and regulations and review and discuss with management the Compensation Discussion & Analysis (CD&A) required by the SEC and recommend to the board that the CD&A be included in the company's annual proxy statement
- Oversee and evaluate the company's overall human resources and compensation structure, policies and programs including the implementation and progress of the company's inclusion and diversity initiatives
- Conduct an annual evaluation of the committee's performance and report on the committee's activities at each meeting of the entire board of directors

Compensation Philosophy

The compensation and organizational development committee plays an essential role in setting the overall tone for the company's philosophy with respect to rewards and incentives generally and executive compensation in particular. Among other things, the members of the committee are expected to continuously review and assess the company's executive compensation philosophy and provide counsel and guidance to the CEO and leaders of the human resources function with respect to alternative approaches to rewarding employees for the work they perform on behalf of the company.

When preparing the statement of the company's executive compensation philosophy the committee should begin with a description of the primary purposes of the executive compensation program, such as attracting, retaining and rewarding talented leaders who can achieve sustainable and profitable growth for the company's businesses and maximize the long-term value of the company for its shareholders and other stakeholders. The statement of philosophy is often broken out into several categories, each of which are considered to be important for recruiting and retaining the best people to lead the organization. For example, realizing that qualified and experienced leaders are highly sought after it is essential that companies be prepared to offer compensation packages that are competitive, which means that the statement of philosophy should incorporate regular comparison of the company's total compensation levels against comparable companies in each of the industries from which the company is likely to draw executive talent, establishing target amounts for each element of compensation that are based on values reported by the company's comparator group; and considering factors related to the executive's potential impact on the company's results, scope of responsibility and accountability and reporting structure.

Compensation plans must also motivate executives to consistently deliver superior performance and this means ensuring that executives have a significant proportion of total annual compensation contingent upon achieving objective measures of financial and operating performance; establishing an appropriate "mix" of compensation elements to ensure an appropriate and balanced focus on short- and long-term results; and preserving a strong and direct relationship between business and individual performance, and the short- and long-term compensation earned by executives. Committees should strive to create incentive arrangements that provide executives with opportunities to achieve compensation levels comparable with the highest earners among their peers at other companies; however, incentives should be tailored so that they are aligned with the company's long-term strategic objectives and not just winning compensation battles with competitors.

Finally, the compensation package should be built in a way that ensures that executives are properly engaged with the pursuit and achievement of the company's long-term strategic goals and meeting the expectations of the company's stakeholders. Engagement provides a foundation for building a deep and committed relationship between the executive and the company and makes the executive a stronger ambassador of the company to both internal and external stakeholders. In order to achieve engagement, the company's executive compensation philosophy must include linking a material portion of executive compensation to measures of business performance for which the executive has direct line of sight and accountability; ensuring that the company's compensation programs and practices encourage appropriate risk taking and discourage inappropriate risk taking; and ensuring that senior executives meaningfully share the risks and rewards of ownership with the company's shareholders by basing a portion of their total compensation on share price performance. While compensation arrangements have traditionally emphasized achievement of financial goals, mounting pressure from institutional investors and other stakeholders has driven companies to include sustainability issues in their executive compensation philosophies and explicitly provide that sustainability performance and innovation will be tracked and that a significant element of executive rewards will be based on demonstrable success in those areas.

Executive Compensation

While the compensation and organizational development committee oversees compensation arrangements for everyone inside the company the committee has special duties and responsibilities with respect to the compensation of the CEO and other members of the executive team.[11] One important task of the committee is ensuring that the company has access to the C-suite level talent necessary for it to be successful and this means that committee members must regularly review, no less frequently than annually, competitive market data, including executive compensation surveys and reports compiled by third party consultants, to assess the adequacy and competitiveness of the company's executive compensation plans vis-à-vis the company's peers in the industry with which they may be competing for talent. When considering the compensation of executive officers other than the CEO the committee should take into account the recommendations of the CEO and the head of the company's human resources function. The committee should also advise and consult with the CEO and the head of the company's human resources function on the terms and conditions of any incentive plans for executive officers other than the CEO, mid-year compensation changes for such executives, the terms of employment for all new executives and the termination of employment of any executives. The entire process used by the committee in determining what it considers to be the appropriate level and type of executive compensation should be disclosed in the company's public filings or reports to shareholders and other stakeholders including a report that meets the specifications of the SEC with respect to the required CD&A report.

While the compensation and organizational development committee is responsible for compensation review and assessment for all of the company's executives, CEO performance and compensation is obviously a central issue and concern for the committee. Prior to the start of each fiscal year, the committee and the CEO should discuss the metrics and performance goals for the CEO during the upcoming fiscal year, with metrics and goals being measurable and based on financial results, strategic imperatives and other matters deemed appropriate by the committee and the entire board of directors. The results of these discussions should be ratified by all of the independent directors on the board, not just those members who are assigned to the compensation and organizational development committee.

The committee should also oversee the development of a performance evaluation process for the CEO that typically includes a self-evaluation by the CEO, input from the CEO's direct reports and input from all directors. Efforts should be made to provide the CEO with continuous feedback throughout the year and a formal performance evaluation should be provided to the CEO annually following the fiscal year end and after the performance of the CEO has been reviewed by the committee. The information from the performance evaluation will be used to measure how well the CEO has performed against the previously agreed metrics and performance goals and make decisions on performance actions with respect to the CEO. The compensation and organizational development committee is responsible for consulting with the entire board on CEO compensation actions and communicating to the CEO all compensation actions relating to him or her. In no event shall the CEO be present during discussions and/or voting by the entire board of directors on his/her own compensation actions.

Incentive Compensation Plans

The compensation and organizational development committee should oversee the company's incentive compensation plans. With respect to bonus plans, the committee should approve and have oversight over all such plans and specific authority to designate employees eligible to participate in such plan(s); approve the financial metrics and performance goals under such plan(s); approve the total bonus pool/plan payout; approve individual payouts for executive officers; and delegate authority to management for the day-to-day non-material administration of the plan(s). The committee should also approve and oversee all of the company's stock-based compensation plans and have the authority to make recommendations to the board regarding the adoption, amendment, design parameters and termination of such plans; approve grant guidelines, grant provisions and ongoing share utilization; approve individual grants to executive officers; delegate authority to management to make grants to non-executive officers (including new hires, promotions, annual awards, and for retention purposes); interpret plan provisions when appropriate; designate employees eligible to participate in the plans; and delegate authority to management with respect to the day-to-day non-material administration of the plan(s). Finally, the committee should establish and periodically review and recommend stock ownership guidelines for directors and executives.

Organizational Development

While most of the stated duties and responsibilities of the compensation and organizational development committee relate to executive compensation, not surprisingly given the intense interest in that topic among regulators, investors and other stakeholders, the committee is usually the primary group within the entire board of directors that is tasked with providing support on the following important issues and topics relating to the structure of the company's management team and ensuring that the structure adapts to address changes in the company's operating environment:

- *Management Team Structure:* The committee should regularly consult with the CEO regarding the establishment of senior management positions and provide direction for management in the recruitment for such positions; however, the actual hiring and termination of senior managers should generally be left to the discretion of the CEO with appropriate consultation from the committee.
- *CEO:* The committee should provide input to the entire board of directors from time to time relating to the employment and disengagement of the CEO, and also should, as appropriate, assist the board in recruiting candidates for the CEO position.
- *Management Succession and Development Planning:* The committee plays an important role in the critical areas of management succession (including CEO succession), management development at all levels and management retention at all levels. The committee should be responsible for ensuring that there are current and viable back-up and succession plans for the CEO and each of the key members of the executive team and that there are specific development programs in place to minimize any loss of time or effectiveness in transitions from a current officer to a successor. The committee should review these plans no less frequently than annually and provide guidance to management, and the entire board of directors, regarding any weaknesses in the plans identified by the committee.
- *Leadership Development:* The compensation and organizational development committee should be responsible for providing guidance to the CEO and the executive leader of the company's human resources function relating to leading development including global talent and organization reviews, leadership assessments, performance reviews, recruiting, leadership training programs, development of the company's talent pipeline and development of alumni networks.

Beyond the specific matters above, the compensation and organizational committee should meet periodically to review and discuss all of the company's organizational and human resources practices and policies to ensure that they are effective tools for strengthening the organization and aligned with the company's overall strategy.

Sustainability Performance

It is no secret that incentive elements of executive compensation arrangements have long been tied to financial performance and increasing shareholder value as demonstrated by improvements in share prices.

Certainly financial success is important to the long-term viability of the business and provides the CEO and other senior executives with access to the capital necessary to remain competitive and pursue and commercialize innovative products, services and technologies; however, there is growing interest among stakeholders, including many institutional investors still very interested in financial returns, to create links between executive compensation and sustainability measures (i.e., metrics based on ESG targets). A Global Compact publication recommended that the duties and responsibilities of the compensation committee include:[12]

- Ensuring that sustainability issues are included in the compensation philosophy (e.g., the intent to reward sustainability performance and innovation, pay a living wage, ensure equitable pay, ensure appropriate CEO to worker pay ratios and limit excessive compensation, etc.)
- Drafting a CEO position profile/description that includes reference to sustainability experience, values and leadership, fostering a sustainability culture, incorporating sustainability into corporate strategies and enterprise risk management, ensuring effective internal controls and management systems for sustainability and maintaining quality stakeholder relationships
- Mandating that the CEO's annual performance plan and evaluation/ review include sustainability objectives, leadership and competencies
- Implementing succession planning and management/leadership development programs that include sustainability competencies, leadership and values alignment; incorporate sustainability as a factor in position profiles, development plans and career planning for executive leadership and potential successors; and integrate sustainability into talent management strategies and discussions

While a strong business case can be made for including sustainability in the overall strategic goals and objectives for a company and, in turn, integrating sustainability into the elements of executive compensation, it is still far from settled practice. In fact, surveys conducted by executive compensation consultants among S&P 500 companies have found that only 2% of the companies tied voluntary environmental targets (e.g., reduction of greenhouse gas emissions) to executive compensation and that just 2.6% of the companies had a performance metric tied to diversity.[13] Several practical issues need to be overcome in order for sustainability performance to take a more central role in executive compensation. For example, compensation arrangements become unworkable if they attempt to address too many metrics. According to Burchman and Sullivan, compensation consultants have traditionally recommended that compensation plans focus on no more than five metrics—one or two financial metrics, such as sales growth or earnings per share, and two or three nonfinancial metrics, in areas such as quality or innovation—and cautioned that including additional metrics, such as sustainability, will likely dilute executive focus.[14] Another problem, at least in the U.S., is that regulators have been slow to prioritize sustainability and environmental risks in their pronouncements regarding reporting; however, regulators outside the U.S., notably in Europe, have moved aggressively to formally include sustainability into corporate governance frameworks, voluntary reporting on sustainability has become increasingly prevalent and companies are becoming more sophisticated with respect to integrating sustainability and financial performance in the disclosures they make to their stakeholders. Advances in sustainability reporting provide a foundation for constructing sustainability metrics that can be added to the financial results and measures of quality and innovation.

While the compensation and organizational development committee is the body of the entire board of directors that focuses its efforts on executive compensation, significant actions in that area must still be reviewed and endorsed by all of the directors. Directors have long considered financial performance and long-term shareholder value to be the bedrock of their fiduciary responsibilities; however, in recent years boards have shown a willingness to "explicitly embrace the proposition that sustainability is a core indicator of the CEO's and internal company's responsibilities and performance".[15] The key, according to Burchman and Sullivan, is to focus on those ESG factors that are "relevant to a company's business" rather than attempting to address all seventeen of the SDGs identified by the United Nations.[16] Any ESG factor recommended for inclusion in executive compensation performance metrics must be grounded in a solid business case and accompanied by a clear plan of action with milestones that are reasonably within the scope of the CEO's direct authority—in other words, as explained by Burchman and Sullivan, "well-defined metrics tied to concrete plans". Burchman and Sullivan noted that if companies are not yet able to define a specific sustainability metric, the board can still reasonably incentivize the CEO and other executives to "do no harm" by retaining the right, which should be laid out specifically in the executive compensation policy, to reduce incentive awards in case of substantial damage to the company's business or reputation due to a failure to take adequate precautions (e.g., an oil spill or harm to workers in the supply chain due to malfeasance by the company's supply chain partners that should have been discovered).

The future of linking sustainability performance to executive compensation may be anticipated by observing the steps that have already been taken by a handful of high profile companies around the world, especially firms operating in industries where it is clear that operational activities can and do have significant and visible environmental and social impacts. For these companies it is already fairly straightforward to make the business case for targeted, and relatively easy-to-track, sustainability initiatives such as managing and reducing greenhouse gas emissions and energy or water use, improving workplace diversity and enhancing employee safety. What is needed is for companies to make the pitch to investors that pursuit and achievement of these goals is not only the "right thing to do" from an environmental and/or social perspective but also will reap financial benefits in the form of cost savings, better risk management and a stronger brand that will attract new customers and talented workers. Metrics must be creatively designed given the end results of most sustainability initiatives cannot be learned for many years, often decades after they are first launched. In these situations, executives must be incentivized by rewards that are based on achieving clearly defined interim milestones.[17]

Evaluation of Committee Performance

The committee should conduct an annual evaluation of its performance and effectiveness, which may be a self-evaluation or an evaluation employing such other resources or procedures as the committee may deem appropriate. The committee should also review and reassess its charter on a periodic basis and submit any recommended changes to the board for its consideration. The committee's evaluation process should be coordinated with similar reviews undertaken by the audit and governance committees of the board.

Notes

1 See generally NYSE Listing Manual § 303A.05 and Nasdaq Rules 5605(d) and 5615. Both national securities exchanges provide exemptions for their compensation committee listing standards for similar categories of issuers (e.g., limited partnerships, companies in bankruptcy, closed-end and open-end funds registered under the Investment Company Act of 1940 and controlled companies) and also provide for relaxed standards, not discussed in this section, while listed companies fall within the definition of a "smaller reporting company", which is generally the case when the company's public equity float is less than $250 million).
2 For further discussion, see Glass Lewis, *In-Depth: Linking Compensation to Sustainability* (March 2016), available at https://glasslewis.com.
3 R. Sainty, "Engaging Boards of Directors at the Interface of Corporate Sustainability and Corporate Governance", *Governance Directions* (March 2016), 85, 87.
4 Nasdaq listing standards allow smaller reporting companies to adopt either a formal written compensation committee charter or a board resolution that covers only a specified portion of the items that need to be addressed in the charters of larger companies. For examples of compensation and organizational development committee charters and additional commentary on preparation of such charters, see "Board Committee Charters" in the management tools available as part of "Governance: A Library of Resources for Sustainable Entrepreneurs" prepared and distributed by the Sustainable Entrepreneurship Project (www.seproject.org).

5 *The Essential Role of the Corporate Secretary to Enhance Board Sustainability Oversight: A Best Practices Guide* (United Nations Global Compact, September 2016).

6 NYSE Listing Manual § 303A.05(a).

7 Nasdaq Listing Rule 5605(d)(1).

8 Nasdaq Listing Rule 5605(a)(1).

9 Nasdaq Listing Rule 5605(d)(2).

10 Nasdaq Listing Rule 5605(d)(3).

11 The rules and regulations relating to compensation committees have been supplemented by mandates for increased shareholder involvement in consideration and approval of executive compensation. See generally NYSE Listing Manual § 303A.08 (requiring NYSE-listed companies to provide their shareholders with the opportunity to vote on all equity compensation plans and material revisions thereto, with limited exceptions).

12 *The Essential Role of the Corporate Secretary to Enhance Board Sustainability Oversight: A Best Practices Guide* (United Nations Global Compact, September 2016).

13 S. Burchman and B. Sullivan, "It's Time to Tie Executive Compensation to Sustainability", *Harvard Business Review* (August 17, 2017), available at https://hbr.org/2017/08/its-time-to-tie-executive-compensation-to-sustainability (accessed May 13, 2020). Larsen cited a report published in 2015 by the sustainability non-profit Ceres along with Sustainalytics that found that 24% of the 613 largest publicly traded companies tied some aspect of sustainability to executive compensation; however, a majority of the sustainability initiatives in the report were related to compliance matters as to which the company was already required to disclose and that only 3% of the companies linked executive compensation to voluntary sustainability performance targets. K. Larsen, "Why tying CEO pay to sustainability still isn't a slam dunk", *GreenBiz* (May 26, 2015), available at www.greenbiz.com/article/why-tying-ceo-pay-sustainability-still-isnt-slam-dunk (accessed May 13, 2020).

14 Id.

15 Id. (quoting Bennett Freeman, former senior vice president for social research and policy of the Calvert Group, who actually argued that director acceptance of sustainability as a core indicator of performance would proceed quite slowly).

16 S. Burchman and B. Sullivan, "It's Time to Tie Executive Compensation to Sustainability", *Harvard Business Review* (August 17, 2017), available at https://hbr.org/2017/08/its-time-to-tie-executive-compensation-to-sustainability (accessed May 13, 2020).

17 For discussion of empirical research on the integration of sustainability performance into executive compensation, see *In-Depth: Linking Compensation to Sustainability* (San Francisco: Glass Lewis, March 2016).

7 Corporate Social Responsibility Committee

While CSR and corporate sustainability need to have an important place on the agenda for full board meetings, larger companies typically rely on one or more committees when it comes to allocating specific tasks and tapping into specialized resources and expertise.[1] One approach that is growing in popularity is the creation of public policy/CSR, social and cultural responsibility and/or environmental responsibility, health, safety and technology committees composed of a sub-group of the entire board that is charged with focusing more time and effort on sustainability generally and important topics within sustainability.[2] While other board committees focus on internal controls, financial disclosure and reporting, and the procedures of board and committee activities, CSR committees concentrate on strategies for ensuring that the company is seen as a good "corporate citizen". A committee of this type is seen as important in light of the downturn in the public's trust of corporations due to the recent accounting scandals.

Global Compact LEAD argued that there are a number of reasons why companies, at least during the early stages as they begin to deal with corporate sustainability, may actually benefit from the establishment of a standalone committee at the board level focusing on sustainability.[3] For example, it significantly increases the amount of time that board members can dedicate to these discussions and increases the visibility of the board's commitment, thus sending an important signal to both internal and external stakeholders. On the other hand, boards need to be careful that relying on a separate committee reduces the uptake of sustainability by all of the directors and hampers integration into other functional committees. Global Compact LEAD observed that directors serving on a sustainability committee must carry significant weight and have a high standing on the board in order to ensure that committee decisions are given high priority throughout the boardroom, a factor that has led to the appointment of the chairperson of the board to sustainability committees, and that a high degree of interaction between this committee and the other specialized committees with relevant responsibilities should be ensured to increase coordination and maximize synergies. Coordination among committees can be enhanced by having representatives of other relevant committees, as well as the board chairperson, serve on the sustainability committee. The role of the committee will likely evolve as time goes by and the committee may actually be dissolved at the point where sustainability has been fully embedded in the mindsets and deliberations of all of the directors. Even if the committee does remain in place, its role may be that of a "coordinator", with strategies, commitments and targets being set by the entire board and the committee providing support with the assistance of an internal sustainability office.

It is important to remember that a CSR committee of the board of directors must be placed within the context of the company's broader processes for governance of corporate responsibility, all of which should be initiated by the entire board of directors.

While the discussion below assumes that the board-level committee focused on CSR and sustainability is composed entirely of board members, some companies have opted for "mixed" committees that directly involved non-director participants. For example, a company may form a committee to make recommendations to the board regarding CSR and sustainability strategy that includes a range of participants starting with the chairperson of the board, who also would chair this committee, the CEO and several other members of the executive team, several independent board members and, very importantly, a select group of independent committee members who are not directors of the company but can provide advice and feedback on specific issues and/or from key stakeholder groups. A committee such as this one, as well as any CSR committee composed solely of directors, may also have support from other formalized committees or groups: an operating committee composed of all the top executives and at least one member of the board-level CSR committee, typically the chairperson of that committee, that will establish policies and processes on CSR, environment, ethics and business practice, procurement, employment and health and safety standards; a reporting and disclosure committee responsible for establishing and monitoring performance standards and recommendations regarding reporting practices; and a community investment and development committee focused on employee and community engagement.

Charter and Activities of Corporate Responsibility Committee

The CSR committee should have a charter, developed through extensive discussions by all of the members of the board, that demarcates the duties and responsibilities of the committee and its relationship to the entire board, other board committees, the management team and the stakeholders of the company. There is no universal template for a CSR committee charter; however, it is recommended that the drafters consider including provisions that describe the overall purpose of the committee; relevant guidelines with respect to composition and procedures; the duties and responsibilities of the committee; the rights and expectations of committee members regarding support for the committee's activities; and procedures for regularly assessing the performance of the committee and, as necessary, making changes to the charter.[4] Some of the unique topics that might be covered in such a charter include review of various activities relating to the promotion of the company's public image, including advertising, community relations and charitable contributions; review of company policies and programs relating to ensuring compliance with laws and regulations involving the environment, safety and health; review and consideration of company involvement in claims and litigations; and review and evaluation of the company's legal compliance programs and oversight of the activities of the company's chief compliance officer. The corporate responsibility committee is sometimes referred to as the corporate compliance committee, although many companies are separating social responsibility from compliance given that social responsibility is typically "regulated" through voluntary standards rather than "hard law".

Statement of Purpose

The CSR committee charter should open with a statement of the purpose of the committee, which should be based on the assessment of the entire board regarding the role that the committee will play in the governance of CSR and sustainability issues. Different approaches to drafting the statement of purpose can be found. For example, the purpose of the committee may be stated simply as assisting the board in overseeing the company's activities in the area of corporate responsibility; however, many charters include more details such as participating in the development and implementation of sustainability positions and commitments, promoting a corporate culture that values sustainability, reviewing performance against sustainability goals and ensuring that the board considers the impact on all stakeholders when setting strategy and making decisions about operational activities. If applicable, the charter should state that the committee was formed in order to comply with the requirements of regulations or listing standards applicable to the company. If necessary, the charter may make it clear that certain other activities that may be related to corporate responsibility may be under the scope of responsibility for other committees (e.g., the audit committee typically retains primary responsibility for financial reporting, financial audit matters and internal controls over financial reporting). In addition, the charter should make it clear that the committee will have the authority to undertake the specific duties and responsibilities described in the charter and such other duties as are assigned by law, the company's charter documents or by the entire board.

Composition, Meetings and Procedures

The charter should describe the composition of the committee including the number of members and any specific qualifications for membership that the board elects to adopt. Typically all, or a majority, of the members of the committee should be determined to be "independent" in accordance with the company's corporate governance guidelines. One of the members of the committee should be designated by the board as the chair of the committee and the service of all of the members and the position of committee chair should be at the pleasure of the board and be subject to annual consideration for appointment by the board on the recommendation of the board's governance and nominating committee. Companies take different approaches regarding the role and responsibilities of the chairperson of the CSR committee. In general, the preferred approach is to select someone who is able and willing to assume a high profile role within and outside the company with respect to the management and explanation of the company's CSR commitments and activities.

Beyond "independence", relevant considerations with respect to the composition of the CSR committee include skills, experience and expertise in the areas of sustainability that are most relevant to the company's operations and CSR commitments and diversity with respect to skills, ethnicity, cultural background and age, itself a hallmark of effective social responsibility. The nomination and governance committee of the board should develop a matrix of sustainability skills that can be applied when considering candidates for the entire board and membership on the CSR committee. For example, at least one member of the committee should have demonstrated skills/experience in corporate sustainability including perhaps an executive with a successful track record on sustainability or a topic expert. With regard to diversity, it is essential that the CSR committee include members who can contribute experiences from a broad range of viewpoints including gender and ethnic diversity and experiences living and working among the communities in which the company is operating.

The charter should specify the minimum number of meetings of the committee to be held annually. In general, CSR committees should meet at least four times a year, with meetings generally scheduled to coincide with meetings of the entire board of directors; however, provision should be made for special meetings at the call of the chair of the committee or two or more of the members of the committee. Some charters provide that the committee may form subcommittees for any purpose and may delegate to such subcommittees or to members of the company's management such powers and authority as it deems appropriate. Since committees are bodies that make decisions and recommendations from time to time, the charter should address voting procedures and the authority, if given, of the chairperson to resolve deadlocks.

The committee may adopt, either in the charter or in separate operating guidelines, procedures for handling issues and activities that commonly come before the committee. For example, if the committee will be reviewing proposals from outside parties for company support of activities within the committee's areas of interest then it should consider adopting guidelines with respect to the information required from third parties (i.e., activities and track record of the organization; budget for the proposed activity; goals and performance metrics for assessing the impact of the activity); the due diligence procedures to be followed by the committee; the criteria for approval of proposals; ratification of committee approvals by the entire board; monitoring of the disbursement and use of company resources; and evaluation of the project and reporting on results to the entire board. The guidelines should be supplemented by "standardized" documentation for approved proposals that include the safeguards that have been identified by the committee.

Provision should be made for the committee to have the appropriate resources and authority to discharge its responsibilities, including the sole authority, as it deems appropriate, to select, retain and terminate the engagement of such outside consultants and counsel to independently advise it as the committee may deem necessary or helpful in carrying out its responsibilities and to establish the fees and other terms for the retention of such consultants and counsel, such fees to be borne by the company. Adequate resources for the committee should include support by the member of the executive team who has been assigned responsibility for oversight of the company's sustainability activities. Companies often will create a chief sustainability officer (CSO) position and the committee should work closely with the CEO and other members of the executive team on recruiting and hiring the CSO and determining the qualifications and responsibilities associated with the position. Committee members should meet regularly with the CSO and, at the discretion of the chair of the committee, the company's management and staff. The committee should also meet periodically with the CSO in a separate executive session to discuss such matters as the committee members believe should be considered privately.

The committee should maintain written minutes or other records of its meetings and activities and the chair of the committee should report to the board following meetings of the committee, and as otherwise requested by the chairperson of the board. The format of presentations should be established by the entire board and sufficient time should be set aside at meetings of the entire board to ensure that all members are fully briefed on important sustainability issues. The CSR committee can and should make recommendations to the chairperson of the entire board regarding appropriate training on sustainability topics that should be included in the development curriculum for all of the directors, not just members of the CSR committee.

Scope of Committee Duties and Responsibilities

The CSR committee charter must include a description of the intended scope of the committee's duties and responsibility. The committee's role will depend on a variety of factors including the extent to which the entire board has reserved primary authority on sustainability topics and the degree to which the company relies on non-board bodies, such as a CSR steering committee, to oversee particular CSR projects. Regardless of how responsibilities may be allocated among the company's various governance groups, it is essential that attention be paid to fundamental activities and topics such as development and implementation of sustainability strategy, innovation, climate change, human rights, political spending, diversity, stakeholder engagement, management engagement, supply chain management and transparency and disclosure.

One study found that while some companies simply referred to "social issues" or to a single issue such as "political contributions" or "charitable contributions", most companies had more detailed descriptions of the duties of committees assigned to oversee social issues that included activities such as the following:[5]

- Reviewing and updating the company's human rights policy and monitoring reports from management regarding ongoing compliance programs relating to the policy and any reports of possible human rights violations
- Reviewing and updating the company's safety and health policy and overseeing all safety programs instituted by the company
- Monitoring regular reports from management regarding ongoing compliance with the company's safety programs and compliance with applicable safety laws and regulations
- Reviewing and updating the company's community health programs and any public health and medical issues that may affect personnel assigned to any operating location
- Reviewing and updating the company's community policy and overseeing all governmental and stakeholder relations, and social investment and sustainable development programs, including reports on these programs from management
- Reviewing and updating the company's political activity and spending practices statement and overseeing the company's political activity and spending practices, including annual disclosure of the company's political contributions and those of company-affiliated political action committees
- Overseeing the company's position and practices on other significant issues of corporate public responsibility such as workforce diversity, data privacy and government affairs strategies (including lobbying activities)

In a December 2016 report on how board committees among S&P 500 companies had evolved to address new challenges, the EY Center for Board Matters noted that CSR committees of the board were generally responsible for reviewing the company's policies and practices related to specific public issues of concern to shareholders, the company, employees, communities served and the general public, with oversight of corporate responsibility, environmental sustainability, diversity and inclusiveness, and/or brand management efforts. The functions of the committee might overlap with the board's public policy and compliance committees. The sectors most likely to have a CSR committee included financial services, consumer discretionary and materials.[6]

The description of committee responsibilities in the charter generally begins with a broad statement that the committee will be responsible for evaluating emerging social, political and environmental trends, issues and concerns that affect or could affect the company's business activities and performance; and making recommendations to the board and management regarding how the business can adjust to these trends. In other words, the committee should be the "eyes and ears" of the board with respect to sustainability trends and issues, although all members of the board should be educated with respect to sustainability and its role in the long-term strategy of the company. The committee should also be charged with overseeing the company's activities in the area of corporate responsibility and sustainability that may have an impact on the company's business operations or public image, in light of political and social trends and public policy issues. In addition, the committee should be the primary group within the board with respect to assessing management's implementation of the corporate responsibility and sustainability programs and overseeing the company's participation in external CSR standards or instruments such as the UN Global Compact. The charter will list the key topics of concern for the committee, which should be tailored to the specific circumstances of the company as opposed to a "boilerplate" list. Common topics include strategic philanthropy, charitable contributions and employee community involvement including funding of CSR activities of third parties within a budget determined by the board; public policy and advocacy, including lobbying, political contributions and public policy positions with respect to pending legislative or other initiatives; environmental management; supply chain management; human rights, as reflected in the company's policies and actions toward employees, suppliers, clients and communities; CSR governance and reporting; and compliance and risk management.

The list and description of the duties and responsibilities in the charter may be supplemented by identification of specific areas of interest, consistent with the overriding CSR commitments of the company adopted by the board, within which CSR activities may be conducted, such as the following:

- Eradicating hunger, poverty and malnutrition, promoting health care including preventive health care and sanitation and making available safe drinking water;
- Promoting education, including special education and employment-enhancing vocational skills especially among children, women, the elderly and the differently abled and livelihood enhancement projects;
- Promoting gender equality, empowering women, setting up homes and hostels for women and orphans; setting up old age homes, day care centers and such other facilities for senior citizens and measures for reducing inequalities faced by socially and economically backward groups;
- Ensuring environmental sustainability, ecological balance, protection of flora and fauna, animal welfare, agro forestry, conservation of natural resources and maintaining quality of soil, air and water; and
- Protection of national heritage, art and culture including restoration of buildings and sites of historical importance and works of art; setting up public libraries; promotion and development of traditional arts and handicrafts.

An important role for the CSR committee is acting as the focal point of the board's efforts to oversee the company's activities with respect to stakeholder engagement. Corporate sustainability requires that companies engage with all of their stakeholders, not just investors, on a wide range of issues in order to better understand the needs and expectations of stakeholders with respect to the company's operational activities and specific initiatives with respect to environmental and social responsibility. Members of the CSR committee should be selected based, at least in part, on their experience in stakeholder engagement and their reputation and network within key stakeholder groups. As part of discharging its responsibilities for overseeing preparation and distribution of the company's annual reports on CSR and sustainability the CSR committee should ensure that the mechanisms used for engagement and communication with each of the stakeholder types are carefully described and that a candid assessment of stakeholder relations is included in the report.

Companies have begun to adopt formal policies relating to stakeholder engagement and community development, particularly in those instances where the company's operations can reasonably be expected to have a significant environmental impact on the surrounding communities (e.g., oil and gas production and other extractive industries). A variety of ideas and principles may be expressed in a stakeholder engagement policy. First and foremost should be the concept of transparency and a commitment by the company to disclose the material terms of its operational activities in the community and the environmental, social and economic objectives that the company is pursuing through those activities. Another essential guiding principle for this type of policy is, of course, a commitment to engaging and consulting with community representatives, and all stakeholders, as part of the process of deciding whether or not to proceed with material activities that might have a material impact on the community and/or one or more other stakeholders. The goal of consultation should be to assess and, where necessary and practicable, implement measures to avoid or mitigate adverse environmental or social impacts. The company should commit to keeping abreast of the concerns and perspectives of stakeholders and keeping them informed of plans in order to ensure continuous engagement and open communications. Other topics that should be addressed in the policy include managing impacts, social investment priorities, supplier performance and local content, procedures for addressing complaints and grievances, and accountability and review. Finally, the policy should spell out the process by which community members and other stakeholders may submit grievances and have them promptly and fairly addressed by company and should provide for designation of personnel who will be held accountable for implementation of the policy and for regular monitoring and review of the policy.

The CSR committee should also be responsible for engaging with the CEO and other members of the executive team on sustainability topics of interest to the general public and on the actions that management is taking to accomplish the company's CSR strategy and goals. Engagement can include regular informal meeting as well as formal presentations on diversity matters, policies of importance to customers and consumers, charitable contributions, legislative and regulatory issues affecting the company, health and wellbeing trends, and other environmental, philanthropic or legal issues of particular public interest including progress toward the company's publicly stated CSR goals. As necessary and appropriate, the CSR committee should meet with leaders of business units or departments responsible for specific sustainability topics (e.g., meetings with the company's human rights department regarding human rights matters of significance to the company). The CSR committee should also ensure that the CEO and other members of the executive team should set aside time on a regular basis, perhaps every two or three months, to come together for a focused meeting on CSR and sustainability issues to ensure that they are adequately implementing the company's CSR strategies and providing the requisite leadership with respect to sustainability. The goal of these meetings is to ensure that environmental and social issues are integrated consistently into the day-to-day activities of each of the company's business units and departments. Reports on all such meetings should be delivered to the CSR committee.

When drafting and implementing processes related to the duties and responsibilities of the CSR committee consideration should also be given to sustainability-related activities and issues that may have been assigned to other standing committees of the board. For example, the compliance and risk management committee, as well as the audit committee, will be involved in oversight of risks related to sustainability issues and compliance with binding and non-binding standards; the governance and nominating committee should integrate sustainability criteria into selection of directors and include sustainability topics in director development programs; and the compensation committee should integrate sustainability criteria into executive compensation and review.[7] The chairperson of the CSR committee should maintain clear and continuous communications with other committees to ensure that board consideration of all sustainability-related issues remains coordinated.

Evaluation of Committee Performance

The committee should conduct an annual evaluation of its performance and effectiveness, which may be a self-evaluation or an evaluation employing such other resources or procedures as the committee may deem appropriate. The committee should also review and reassess its charter on a periodic basis and submit any recommended changes to the board for its consideration. A number of assessment tools that boards, CSR committees and individual directors can use with respect to oversight of sustainability have been created in recent years. One example provided by Canadian Business for Social Responsibility included the following questions:[8]

- Has the board developed a common understanding of the business case for sustainability and is that business case reviewed on a regular basis, no less frequently than annually?
- Has the board and management reached agreement on a common definition of CSR and has the company's commitment to CSR as so defined been explicitly communicated among the company's stakeholders?
- Has the board and management developed a CSR vision for the company and incorporated CSR into the company's overall mission and values and the company's code of conduct and ethics?
- Is the board aware of the significant CSR-related issues that are relevant to the company's business and the industries in which the company operates and are those issues incorporated into the company's long-term strategies?
- Has the board established a formal framework for conducting its oversight of sustainability including designation of committees with responsibility for CSR and appointment of an executive officer for CSR activities with a reporting relationship to the board?
- Does the board regularly review progress on the company's performance with respect to CSR goals, objectives and targets?
- Is CSR included as a factor in recruitment of the CEO and other executive officers and is compensation of the executive linked to performance on CSR goals and targets?

- Has the board ensured that material CSR risks are considered with the company's enterprise risk management program?
- Does the board have a means to identify the CSR impacts of its decisions and are CSR impacts, issues and opportunities explicitly considered when approving major decisions?
- Does the board review its own practices to reduce the social and environmental impacts of board meetings?
- Does the board receive unfiltered information on stakeholder issues and concerns?
- Has the board implemented auditing procedures to assess the extent to which the company's CSR commitments are adhered to across the company and within the company's supply chain?
- Is the board's composition and skill set consistent with a strong commitment to sustainability, meaning that the membership of the board reflects the cultural and gender diversity of the marketplace and candidates for directorship are required to have CSR skills, knowledge and experience?
- Does the board's new director orientation process and ongoing professional development program include CSR-related skills?
- Has the board ensured that the company has a formal external reporting program that covers material CSR issues and is the board actively involved in management's assessment of which such issues should be reported and how?
- Does the board approve the company's CSR reporting to stakeholders and do those reports include a message from the chairperson of the board?

Alternative Structures

While this chapter focuses on the duties and activities of a standalone board committee dedicated to CSR and sustainability, companies may attempt to tap into the necessary expertise within and outside the company using alternative structures. For example, the board of directors may create a sustainability steering committee to assume responsibility for managing and coordinating sustainability activities while reserving bigger issues such as setting CSR and sustainability strategy, goals and commitments for the entire board. The steering committee would be chaired by the CSO or another leader from the executive team such as the head of the company's environmental, health and safety (EH&S) activities and would be composed of the executive leaders of all of the business units and departments involved in the CSR and sustainability initiatives (e.g., EH&S, human resources, communications, government and public policy, investor relations, philanthropy, product development, procurement and disclosure and reporting). Additional input for the steering committee would come from various advisory boards composed of representatives of the company's key stakeholders and outside experts who can provide the steering committee with advice based on practical experience and academic research. The primary purpose of the steering committee would be to brief the CEO and relevant committees of the board (e.g., audit, risk and compliance, governance and nominating, and compensation) on sustainability-related issues; however, the mandate of the committee is often expanded to include oversight of major sustainability-focused initiatives and projects.

Notes

1 *A New Agenda for the Board of Directors: Adoption and Oversight of Corporate Sustainability* (Global Compact LEAD, 2012).
2 For further discussion of environmental, health and safety committees, see Chapter 8 (Environmental Responsibility, Health and Safety Committee) in this volume.
3 *A New Agenda for the Board of Directors: Adoption and Oversight of Corporate Sustainability* (Global Compact LEAD, 2012), 14.
4 For examples of CSR committee charters and additional commentary on preparation of such charters, see "Board Committee Charters" in the management tools available as part of "Governance: A Library of Resources for Sustainable Entrepreneurs" prepared and distributed by the Sustainable Entrepreneurship Project (www.seproject.org).
5 P. DeSimone, *Board Oversight of Sustainability Issues: A Study of the S&P 500* (IRRC Institute, March 2014), 1, 13–14.
6 www.ey.com/Publication/vwLUAssets/EY-board-committees-evolve-to-address-new-challenges/$FILE/EY-board-committees-evolve-to-address-new-challenges.pdf.
7 *A New Agenda for the Board of Directors: Adoption and Oversight of Corporate Sustainability* (Global Compact LEAD, 2012), 13.
8 *CSR Governance Guidelines* (Canadian Business for Social Responsibility, 2010).

8 Environmental, Health and Safety Committee

Studies have found that a growing number of companies have implemented board oversight of EH&S, with most of them emphasizing establishment of EH&S management systems to ensure compliance with company policies and related legislation and regulations.[1] In many cases, companies describe environmental oversight broadly and refrain from mentioning specific issues such as climate change or water use. However, some companies are very specific about ensuring that their board-level EH&S committee focuses on policies and management systems; performance and disclosure; related administrative, regulatory and judicial proceedings; public policy strategies; product stewardship; and effects on and relations with communities.

Companies often include "macro" issues relating to the environment, such as climate change, waste management and the impact of a company's operational activities on natural resources, under the general umbrella of EH&S. In addition, EH&S typically refers to compliance with laws and regulations, as well as emerging voluntary standards, relating to environmental protection, health and safety in the workplace, particularly the wellbeing of employees and members of the communities in which the company physically operates. EH&S laws and regulations vary in scope and complexity across jurisdictions and companies operating in the U.S., for example, must contend with regulations promulgated at the federal, state and local levels. The major regulatory players at the federal level in the U.S. include the Occupational Safety and Health Administration, the Environmental Protection Agency (EPA), the Nuclear Regulatory Commission and the Mining Safety and Health Administration. States often have parallel regulatory bodies and often have laws and regulations pertaining to environmental and safety issues that are more stringent than those that have been implemented at the federal level. Companies operating in global markets will need to comply with local laws, such as the sweeping regulations that have been adopted in the EU.

U.S. regulatory agencies relating to environmental management, such as the EPA, began to emerge in the 1970s, which was the same time that workplace safety and occupational health was growing in importance following the passage of the federal Occupational Safety and Health Act in 1970, and by the 1990s companies were responding by creating new departments to address compliance issues relating to EH&S laws and regulations. At the same time, companies were making investments in equipment and personnel to modify existing facilities and manufacturing processes to comply with EH&S regulations and to ensure that new facilities and processes would also be compliant. New technologies allowed companies to establish systems for monitoring and measuring performance against EH&S metrics. At the same time, new EH&S management roles within organizations developed and EH&S management became a recognized professional discipline with its own unique career paths, typically starting in one of the three sub-disciplines, and education and training criterion. While EH&S began as a compliance-focused area, increased interest in sustainability after the turn of the century led to the extension of the portfolio of EH&S leaders beyond compliance into environmental and social responsibility including climate change, energy and water conservation, recycling, wellness, public health, supply chain management and stakeholder engagement.

Environmental, Health and Safety Governance and Management

EH&S concerns, principles and procedures should be integrated into the way that companies are governed and the management systems that are used to control and track day-to-day activities. The board of directors, either directly or through the EH&S committee of the board, should work with senior management to ensure that the company has properly designed and effectively implemented management systems that can support identification of EH&S issues and management of the risks and opportunities associated with those issues. In the environmental area, for example, companies often put in place an environmental management system (EMS) based on ISO 14001, an internationally agreed standard discussed in more detail below which has been praised for its utility in helping companies manage and minimize their environmental impacts, conform to applicable legal requirements and improve their environmental performance through more efficient use of resources and reduction of waste. Key aspects of EH&S governance and management include formulation of EH&S strategy and objectives; adoption, implementation and distribution of an EH&S policy and accompanying EH&S standards; EH&S planning and procedures; creation of an effective EH&S management responsibility framework; EH&S oversight groups at all levels of the organization structure; and audits and site certification.

EH&S Planning and Procedures

In order to properly address EH&S issues associated with the company's operations, appropriate plans and procedures need to be developed under the leadership of senior management with input from all parts of the organization and external stakeholders that may be impacted. In general, implementation and maintenance of EH&S procedures should address EH&S aspects/impacts, hazards, risks, controls and operational changes taking into account the company's current operations and activities and applicable legal obligations. Other factors that need to be considered include the resources that the company can control, aspects that have or can have significant impacts on the company, planned or new developments, new or modified products and services, human behavior, hazards originating outside the workplace, infrastructure and equipment in the workplace and the design of work area processes. Planning and procedures should be conducted based on prioritization of risks and communications with applicable stakeholders.

Management Responsibility for EH&S

Specific management representative(s) should be appointed with the role, responsibilities and authority for ensuring that the company's EH&S policies, programs and procedures are implemented and maintained and reporting on their performance to the board of directors, the EH&S committee and senior executives, including recommendations for improvement whenever necessary. General EH&S responsibilities of the management team include developing the EH&S policy for approval by the board of directors; recommending objectives and targets for EH&S performance and improvement to the board of directors; assigning responsibility and authority for implementation activities; providing the adequate resources needed to implement the policy; ensuring knowledge and skills are developed to effectively apply the EH&S systems and standards; reviewing the EH&S system to ensure its continuing suitability, adequacy, effectiveness; and actively communicating leadership and commitment that is visible to the organization.

Many companies have decided to place senior leadership responsibility for sustainability under the authority of the executive responsible for EH&S. The EH&S executive would be responsible for developing the company's EH&S strategy for consideration and approval by the board of directors and, once the strategy has been approved, ensuring that it is effectively implemented. While a significant portion of the issues that must be considered by the EH&S executive pertain to compliance, more and more companies are looking to EH&S leaders to design and implement strategies that go beyond compliance to include a comprehensive sustainability program. In fact, EH&S leaders are often referred to as the "chief sustainability officer". Regardless of title, the person occupying the position should expect to be responsible for the following:[2]

- Establishing all necessary EH&S programs and procedures to be followed throughout the organization;
- Ensuring that an EH&S management system is established, implemented and maintained in accordance with the requirements of applicable standards, as discussed below;
- Defining, documenting and communicating roles, allocating responsibilities and accountabilities, and delegating authorities to facilitate an effective and efficient EH&S management system;
- Creating successful internal partnerships to integrate EH&S values and practices across the business;
- Communicating enterprise risks associated with EH&S failures;
- Publicly reporting progress on EH&S and sustainability initiatives;
- Engaging with stakeholders and responding to stakeholder inquiries about the company's EH&S and sustainability performance;
- Working with participants in the company's supply chain to ensure they are following appropriate EH&S standards in carrying out their obligations to the company;
- Auditing the company's EH&S initiatives and programs; and
- Reporting regularly to the EH&S committee of the board and other members of the senior management team on the company's EH&S performance and participating in the preparation and dissemination of public reports on the company's EH&S policies, procedures and performance.

The efforts of the EH&S executive should be supported by a formal group or department dedicated to oversight of the company's EH&S programs. The EH&S department should have the authority to issue procedures and rules, and to suspend activities and close facilities or other work areas it deems to be unsafe to people or the environment, or in violation of the company's policies or applicable laws. The EH&S department should be responsible for providing overall guidance on applicable laws and regulations, and working with the departmental safety committees described below to support and maintain an effective EH&S program. The EH&S department also takes the leadership role in preparing and implementing the company's EH&S management systems and continuously assessing the effectiveness of those systems. Other typical duties of an EH&S department include evaluating EH&S risks and developing mitigation strategies; coordinating responses to incidents, investigations, audits and regulatory reviews, as well as managing related filings, reports and licenses; convening safety committees in specific areas where required by law or in keeping with best management practices to develop, implement and enforce health, safety and environmental plans; and ensuring that employees and other stakeholders are engaged in the company's EH&S activities.

EH&S Oversight Committees and Departmental EH&S Committees

While the board of directors and the EH&S committee of the board is responsible for setting the company's overall EH&S strategies and priorities, responsibility for overseeing the implementation of specific EH&S compliance programs will be delegated to one or more EH&S program committees composed of members appointed by senior management with appropriate expertise as indicated by applicable standards and regulations. These committees should include representatives from departments or units that must implement the specific program, as well as a representative from the EH&S department and senior management that has specific education, expertise and professional training in the area being overseen by the particular committee. One of the primary roles of these committees is to review operational programs and identify or develop procedures that meet regulatory compliance and support best EH&S practices. EH&S committees should also establish a means of communication within the company with respect to matters under their oversight, particularly procedures for employees to provide their input and raise their concerns; advise and make recommendations to the EH&S departmental leadership; promote awareness of EH&S issues and ensure that appropriate training and education programs have been implemented; and conduct audits of EH&S compliance and report on the results of such audits to the board of directors, the EH&S committee of the board and senior management.

Charter and Activities of Environment, Health and Safety Committee

The EH&S committee should have a charter that specifies the direct responsibilities of the committee including the review of EH&S regulations; review and approval of company EH&S policies and emergency response plans; and administration of the policies and activities of the company as they relate to the environmental impact of the company's operations and the health, safety and occupational work standards in the workplace in which the company carries on business. The charter should specify the specific duties and powers of the committee and describe the organizational structure of the committee. As with other board committees, the EH&S committee should have the right to appoint independent counsel and should also be obligated to make regular reports to the full board of directors.[3]

Statement of Purpose

The EH&S charter typically begins with a statement of the purpose and role of the EH&S committee. For example, the charter may provide that that the committee has been established to assist the board in discharging the board's responsibilities relating to the company's EH&S policy, procedures and performance. The purpose provision may go on to include various direct duties and responsibilities of the EH&S committee such as reviewing EH&S regulations; reviewing and monitoring environmental policies and obligations that might arise as a result of the business and operations of the company; reviewing and monitoring the policies and activities of the company as they relate to health, safety and occupational work standards in the workplace in which the company carries on business; reviewing and approving the company's EH&S policies and emergency response plans; reviewing EH&S risks and ensuring proper management of those risks; reviewing company compliance, performance and metrics regarding EH&S regulations and matters, and driving continuous improvement and corrective actions to improve performance and compliance; and reviewing the committee charter and making changes as necessary. As a general matter, the EH&S committee charter should make it clear that the committee's overall purpose is to ensure that the company's policies and procedures meet the obligations of the board to achieve regulatory compliance and meet or exceed acceptable industry standards with respect to EH&S matters.

Composition, Meetings and Procedures

The EH&S committee charter should address composition, frequency of meetings, powers and authority of the committee and other procedures. In general, while the same "independence" requirements that apply to audit, governance and compensation committees are not explicitly imposed on EH&S committee members, it is important that the members of the committee be generally familiar with EH&S issues applicable to the company's specific line of business and operational activities. The charter should provide that in addition to the powers and responsibilities expressly delegated to the committee in the charter, the committee should have the authority to exercise any other powers and carry out any other responsibilities from time to time delegated to it by the board. The committee should also be able to conduct or authorize investigations into any matter within the scope of the duties and responsibilities delegated to the committee and have the authority to retain and compensate independent counsel, consultants and other experts and advisors. The board should make it clear in the charter that the company will provide appropriate funding, as determined by the committee, for payment of compensation to any experts or advisors retained by the committee and for payment of ordinary administrative expenses of the committee.

Scope of Duties and Responsibilities

A detailed list of responsibilities for a board committee overseeing EH&S matters might include review and advice to the entire board, other board committees and management with respect to each of the following issues and activities:

- Reviewing reports from management regarding significant events and trends relating to EH&S including significant legislation or regulations, judicial decisions, treaties, protocols, conventions or other agreements, public policies or scientific or technical developments involving EH&S matters that will or may have a material impact on the company's business
- Reviewing reports from management regarding significant risks or exposures faced by the company in the EH&S area, including risks relating to the security of the company's assets and personnel, and steps taken by management to address such risks, and company strategy and initiatives in the area of EH&S
- Monitoring the overall adequacy of the company's EH&S objectives, policies and performance, consistent with prudent industry practices, including processes to ensure compliance with applicable laws and regulations
- Participating in and assessing efforts to advance the company's progress on sustainable development (e.g., for a company engaged in mining operations, the integration of social, environmental and economic principles into the company's operations from exploration through development, operation, reclamation, closure and post closure activities)
- Measuring the effectiveness of internal systems, policies and processes that support achieving the company's EH&S goals, commitments and compliance obligations
- Conducting an annual EH&S management system review that includes a discussion of significant policies and programs, the scope and plans for conducting EH&S and a review of the company's procedures for the handling of EH&S-related complaints and confidential, anonymous employee concerns
- Reviewing and discussing with management material non-compliance by the company with EH&S laws and regulations; and pending or threatened EH&S administrative, regulatory or judicial proceedings that are material to the company, and management's response to such non-compliance and/or proceedings
- Reviewing and evaluating management's responses to significant emerging EH&S issues including public policy, advocacy and stakeholder engagement strategies
- Reviewing the disclosures in the company's required reports to regulators relating to EH&S matters, and periodically reviewing other material public disclosures by the company relating to CSR and sustainable development
- Monitoring significant EH&S public policy, legislative, political and social issues or trends that may materially affect the business

operations, financial performance or public image of the company or industry, and management's response to such matters

- Creating incentive compensation metrics related to EH&S, which would be discussed in the context of providing advice to the compensation committee of the board
- Reviewing product sustainability issues including product stewardship
- Overseeing the management of EH&S risks and the company's interactions relating to EH&S matters with communities, customers and other key stakeholders

EH&S committees may also be asked to meet regularly with management to assess the company's safety and operational compliance practices generally, including assessing the adequacy of the resources, training, communications, risk assessments and auditing of operational processes directed toward supporting safety and operational compliance; assess whether the company's safety and operational compliance practices support the company's ethics codes and policies; and prepare and deliver reports to the full board and management regarding the adequacy and effectiveness of the company's safety and operational compliance programs including recommendations on the substance of such programs and related compliance practices.[4]

Compliance with Laws, Regulations and Standards

Procedures and internal controls need to be developed to evaluate compliance with applicable laws and regulations and other requirements, particularly voluntary standards, to which the company subscribes. Specifically, the EH&S committee of the board should ensure that the company establishes a policy which includes a commitment to compliance with applicable legal and other requirements; establishes, implements and maintains a procedure to identify applicable legal and other requirements; ensures that applicable legal and other requirements are taken into account in the management system; and periodically evaluates the organization's compliance with the applicable legal and other requirements and reports to management on the results of such evaluation.

Supply Chain Management

The company's policies and procedures relating to EH&S should include commitments to inform suppliers, including contractors, of the company's EH&S principles and require them to adopt practices aligned with the company's expectations. Many companies have adopted specific policies and requirements that must be adhered to by contractors when they respond to requests for proposals by the company. For example, a company might require that its contractors:

- Conduct its activities so that equipment, supplies and work practices are safe for workers and can be understood by all workers and others present at the work location
- Provide a safe work area free from recognized hazards, use due care to prevent damage to property materials and equipment, and comply with all applicable federal, state and local EH&S laws, regulations and standards
- Restore to original condition any damaged property, materials and equipment in the company's workplace
- Ensure that all items furnished and all work performed by the contractor comply with the most current applicable requirements of all relevant regulations and standards in the jurisdiction where the work is being performed

Education and Training

Training and awareness are essential to the effectiveness of EH&S programs and procedures. In order to achieve success with respect to their EH&S programs, organizations must ensure that employees are knowledgeable and possess all of the skills, competencies, awareness and behavior necessary to complete their work. The EH&S committee of the board should monitor the efforts of the company to ensure that all persons performing tasks and activities that are under control of the company are competent based on appropriate EH&S education, training or experience. In order for a company to effectively address EH&S issues and ensure that policies and procedures are implemented and followed it is necessary to provide education, information and training to everyone in the organization as well as outside contractors and supply chain partners. It is essential for the EH&S committee of the board to monitor education and training programs and do their best to make sure that all employees are aware of EH&S policies, procedures and requirements and understand their specific roles and responsibilities in achieving conformity with EH&S requirements and the potential consequences of not following procedures.

Stakeholder Engagement

Stakeholder engagement requires implementation of procedures for internal communication among the various levels and functions of the company; communication with contractors and other visitors to the workplace; receiving, documenting and responding to relevant communication from external interested parties; and, as appropriate, external communications regarding the company's significant EH&S aspects and hazards. Engagement with employees is essential for the effectiveness of any EH&S strategy and policy and the EH&S committee of the board should require that senior management establish, implement and maintain procedure for the participation of workers by their involvement in EH&S aspect/hazard identification, risk assessments and determination of controls, incident investigation, and development and review of the company's EH&S policies and objectives; consultation (including contractors, as applicable) where there are any changes that affect EH&S and objectives; and representation on EH&S matters. In addition, relevant external interested parties, such as representatives of the local communities in which the company operates, should be consulted with respect to aspects of the company's activities that might have an adverse EH&S impact on such parties.

Transparency and Disclosure

As interest in CSR and corporate sustainability has grown, companies have found that they are subject to heightened scrutiny and that the traditional disclosure practices that focused primarily, if not exclusively, on financial information and performance and related risks are no longer adequate. Companies must now be prepared to provide disclosures that address the specific concerns and expectations of multiple stakeholders beyond investors including customers, employees, business partners, regulators and activists. This means that the board of directors as a whole, and particularly the members of the EH&S committee, must understand existing and emerging disclosure requirements and ensure that the company has the necessary resources to collect and analyze the required information and present it in a manner that is clear and understandable.

While certain EH&S disclosures have now become minimum legal requirements in some jurisdictions, in general such disclosures are still a voluntary matter and directors have some leeway as to the scope of the disclosure made by their companies and how they are presented to investors and other stakeholders. When establishing a framework for EH&S reporting reference should be made to the topics suggested by the GRI. In the environmental area, the potential topics include materials, energy, water, biodiversity, emissions, effluents and waste, environment compliance and supplier environmental assessment. With regard to occupational health and safety, disclosures should be made on workers' representation in formal joint management–worker health and safety committees; types of injury and rates of injury, occupational diseases, lost days and absenteeism, and number of work-related fatalities; workers with high incidence or high risk of diseases related to their occupation; and health and safety topics covered in formal agreements with trade unions. Disclosures should also be made with respect to the health and safety impacts of product and service categories and incidents of non-compliance concerning the health and safety impacts of products and services. Companies should also be prepared to report on various aspects of their EH&S management system including compliance, risk assessment, objective and target setting, competency and training, communications and consultation, management of change, operational control, monitoring and measurement, self-audit, EH&S program review and emergency preparedness.

Monitoring and Measuring the Effectiveness of EH&S Procedures

One of the primary responsibilities of the EH&S committee is to monitor and measure the effectiveness of the company EH&S policies, programs and procedures. This begins with requiring and receiving regular reports from senior management, as well as other key personnel throughout the company overseeing specific aspects of the company's EH&S programs, and asking tough questions to verify the accuracy of the reports. The reports should be accompanied by data and metrics that have been agreed upon in advance that can be used to quickly identify areas of ongoing concern and progress toward clearly defined goals and objectives. Particular areas of interest include compliance with applicable regulatory and legal requirements and the requirements of any other standards that have been adopted by the company (e.g., ISO 14001 or other management systems schemes), incident investigation, actual and potential non-conformities and corrective/preventive actions. In those instances where the company relies on outside contractors to assist in implementing EH&S programs and procedures, the committee should meet regularly with representatives of those contractors to ascertain contractor performance and, as appropriate, seek and obtain input on the performance of the company's own managers and employees. The committee should ensure that internal audits are scheduled at defined intervals to measure the effectiveness of the company's EH&S programs and procedures including, for example, conformance of the company's EMS to the requirements of ISO 14001. Finally, the committee should work with senior management to develop procedures to establish and maintain records as necessary to monitor performance and determine conformity to the requirements of its EMS and overall EH&S objectives and targets and the results that have been achieved.

The EH&S committee of the board should ensure that a documented process is implemented for regular review of the company's EH&S strategies, policies, procedures and management system by the committee and the company's senior management. Inputs to these reviews should include the following:

- Results of internal audits and evaluations of compliance with applicable legal and other requirements to which the company subscribes
- Results of relevant participation and consultation
- Relevant communication(s) from external interested parties, including complaints
- EH&S performance of the company

- The extent to which EH&S strategic and tactical objectives and targets have been met
- Status of significant incident investigations and corrective/preventive actions
- Follow-up actions from previous management reviews
- Changing circumstances, including developments in legal and other requirements related to the company's EH&S aspects/ hazards
- Technical knowledge and expertise from site-level EH&S professionals
- Recommendations for improvement

The outputs of these reviews should be expected to include possible changes to the company's EH&S policy, objectives, targets, resources and management system. Reviews and audits should provide added value in the form of providing a comprehensive assessment of the adequacy of site risk management, including EH&S and business continuity risks; identifying site management strengths and areas for improvement; identifying "best practices and model programs" that can be disseminated across the organization so that other sites can replicate; and proposing solutions to close gaps identified during the audit process.

Evaluation of Committee Performance

The committee should conduct an annual evaluation of its performance and effectiveness, which may be a self-evaluation or an evaluation employing such other resources or procedures as the committee may deem appropriate. The committee should also review and reassess its charter on a periodic basis and submit any recommended changes to the board for its consideration. Companies will find that there are a number of outside consultants available to assist in evaluating their EH&S programs and performance and make recommendations regarding changes to governance and management processes. In conducting the evaluation, the EH&S committee should focus on ensuring that the committee has been kept aware of the significant EH&S-related issues that are relevant to the company's business and the industries in which the company operates; the company has an adequate formal framework for conducting its oversight of EH&S activities; and the board regularly reviews progress on the company's performance with respect to EH&S goals, objectives and targets. The evaluation process with respect to EH&S issues and performance should be coordinated with similar reviews undertaken by the compliance and risk management committee of the board.[5]

Notes

1   P. DeSimone, *Board Oversight of Sustainability Issues: A Study of the S&P 500* (IRRC Institute, March 2014), 1, 11–12 and 14–15.

2 Adapted from G. Cline, *Adding Sustainability and Quality to EH&S for Manufacturing* (December 5, 2017), available at www.aberdeenessentials.com/opspro-essentials/adding-sustainability-quality-ehs-manufacturing/ (accessed May 12, 2020).

3 For examples of EH&S committee charters and additional commentary on preparation of such charters, see "Board Committee Charters" in the management tools available as part of "Governance: A Library of Resources for Sustainable Entrepreneurs" prepared and distributed by the Sustainable Entrepreneurship Project (www.seproject.org).

4 P. DeSimone, *Board Oversight of Sustainability Issues: A Study of the S&P 500* (IRRC Institute, March 2014), 15.

5 For detailed discussion of compliance and risk management committees, see Chapter 9 (Compliance and Risk Management Committee) in this volume.

9 Compliance and Risk Management Committee

Compliance with laws and regulations applicable to the company's business activities and identifying and managing the risks associated with those activities are two of the fundamental duties and obligations of the board of directors. The emergence of sustainability as a new factor for consideration in boardrooms has expanded the compliance duties to include adherence to voluntary standards that the board has committed to with respect to governance and environmental and social responsibility and broadened the definition of risks to include environmental and social issues and challenges. While creating a separate board committee to focus on compliance and risk management is not a new phenomenon, such committees have grown in importance. Some companies separate compliance and risk management into two different committees; however, in this chapter it is assumed that one committee addresses both topics. It should be noted that companies may place board-level groups assigned to compliance and/or risk management as subcommittees of another standing committee of the board, such as the audit committee. If that approach is taken, the advice in this chapter would apply to such subcommittees. If a compliance and risk management committee is created it should be prepared to coordinate with other board committees such as the audit committee, which brings its expertise in assessing compliance with specified standards, and committees focused on specific regulated issues such as the environmental, health and safety committee.

Compliance and Compliance Programs

In today's business world, all companies, regardless of their size, business model and scope of activities, are required to understand and comply with a plethora of laws and regulations, and the penalties for non-compliance can be significant and often can ruin a company and the careers of the persons involved in the misconduct. For example, criminal sanctions may include fines, probation and remedial action, including restitution, community service and notice to victims. Civil penalties can also be substantial and may include treble damages and the additional costs of litigation. Added to all of this is the damage to the company's reputation and employee morale, and additional scrutiny from government investigators. Finally, companies that have been found to have violated laws in government investigations may be exposed to shareholder lawsuits, loss of business partners, and debarment from government contracting.

In order to fulfill their obligations and avoid the costs associated with violations, all companies should be admonished to adopt and aggressively implement compliance programs in a wide range of areas. Compliance programs are important even for companies that honestly believe they are acting in a lawful fashion, since these programs are probably the best way to establish formal policies and procedures that can guide the actions of employees and institutionalize regular assessment of actual practices. Moreover, the existence of a formal compliance program that is actually followed can be an important factor in reducing the liability of the company in the event that a problem arises in spite of the controls that have been put in place.

Directors' Role in Developing and Overseeing Compliance Programs

When companies run afoul of laws and regulations the publicity can be intense and the adverse reputational and financial consequences to the company are generally quite significant. The post-mortem brings the board of directors to "center stage" and judges, regulators, investors and pundits in the financial press will all be asking whether the directors were paying attention, asking the right questions, adopting and enforcing appropriate policies and procedures, and making it clear that "compliance matters" when setting goals and allocating rewards. Simply put, while directors are not expected to fend off every act of misconduct by executives, employees and agents of their companies, they are responsible for effectively discharging their own duties and responsibilities relating to compliance and ethics programs. While attention to compliance problems is generally most intense for larger, publicly owned companies, directors of firms of all sizes, including privately-owned companies, should consider "compliance" to be a significant part of their jobs. All directors have a fiduciary duty to their corporations and to the stockholders who are actual owners of the corporation and that duty will almost certainly be breached if directors fail to act with care in developing and implementing compliance and ethics programs and as a result the corporation and/or its agents are found to be culpable of misconduct and/or unlawful activity.

Elements of Effective Compliance Programs

In general, a compliance program can be understood to be an internal management system that educates the officers and employees of a company about laws and regulations relevant to the business activities of the company, and establishes processes and procedures to guide and monitor the behavior of those persons. There are no legally mandated standards for compliance programs; however, numerous attempts have been made to identify and define the essential elements of an effective corporate compliance program. In the accounting world, for example, the American Institute of Certified Public Accountants has issued a Statement on Auditing Standards (SAS No. 99, also known as AU 316) "Consideration of Fraud in a Financial Statement Audit", which contains an appendix with examples of measures that companies can use to prevent, deter and detect fraud. The influential U.S. Federal Sentencing Guidelines for Organizational Defendants established by the U.S. Sentencing Commission (Sentencing Guidelines) also identify several areas that should be assessed to determine the effectiveness of a company's efforts to manage its ethical and compliance risks.[1] Specific types of programs, such as those necessary for compliance with export and import laws and regulations, will be influenced by guidelines developed by the agencies chiefly responsible for administration and enforcement in those areas. Finally, there is a rapidly growing body of U.S. case law, notably the *Caremark* case, which is helping to define certain legal principles regarding compliance programs.

Each compliance program should be tailored to the unique circumstances of the company, including the size of the company, the level of regulation applicable to the company's business activities, and its past compliance history. In any case, however, the program should be broad in its scope of application; and extend beyond all officers and employees of the company and its subsidiaries and branches to include outside consultants, advisors, independent contractors and business partners such as distributors, agents, sales representatives, licensees and joint venture partners.

If a company does not have a legal compliance program in place, or has decided to make significant changes to its existing policies and procedures, the first step is coming up with a set of guiding rules and principles for structuring an effective program. There is no shortage of resources in this area, and the right plan for a particular company generally incorporates ideas developed by commentators, other companies in the specific industry and regulatory agencies. In general, companies have based the structure and design of their compliance programs on the recommendations made in the Sentencing Guidelines, the U.S. Sarbanes-Oxley Act of 2002 and guidelines and pronouncements issued by governmental agencies that regulate the activities of the particular business (and, thus, are more likely to be involved in an investigation of wrongdoing by the company). In addition, the growing interest in developing compliance programs and creating of codes of conduct has led to the creation of several websites dedicated to various aspects of business ethics, including the materials made available by organizations such as the Center for Business Ethics, the Corporate Executive Board, the Ethics Resource Center and the Institute for Global Ethics.

Enterprise Risks and Risk Management

No business is without some sort of risk and overcoming those risks is the key to achieving an acceptable return on investment of capital, technology and human resources. Higher levels of risk drive investors to expect greater risk-adjusted returns in exchange for providing capital to the business. The risk profile for each company is different; however, commentators have suggested that the range of risks confronting an enterprise may appear within an extensive list that includes the following, in no particular order: financial markets disruption; credit; interest rate; capital; human resources; transactional; data protection and privacy; legal; enforcement actions by federal or state criminal authorities; Foreign Corrupt Practices Act; governmental investigations; regulatory and compliance requirements; cyberattacks; information technology; business continuity and disaster planning; operational; supply chain; financial disclosure; document retention policies and practices and disclosure (obstruction of justice or civil contempt); executive misconduct or negligence (personal and/or professional); brand; reputational; vendors; business partners; third party service providers; customers; and environmental.[2]

The scope of the potential risks to a company above should illustrate why companies need a formalized approach to risk management, systems and programs that have come to be known as "enterprise risk management", or ERM. ERM programs, which often include compliance aspects or are implemented in conjunction with a separate but related compliance program, have been mandated or highly recommended by federal and state laws and regulations, such as the Sarbanes-Oxley Act of 2002 and the Dodd-Frank Wall Street Reform and Consumer Protection Act; the Sentencing Guidelines; listing standards required by national securities exchanges; credit agencies; directors' and officers' liability insurance carriers; and accounting and audit review standards. In many cases, companies are required, or strongly urged, to create a separate board-level risk management committee and appoint a chief risk officer, a position discussed further below. Apart from legal and regulatory requirements, companies have recognized that ERM can be deployed as an essential business management tool to assess and analyze business and activities on a risk-adjusted basis; engage in sound strategic planning and financial management which requires that all risks of every line of business and activity be assessed and balanced against profitability, and recognize and prepare for the interdependency of events.[3]

A joint report published as a preliminary draft in February 2018 by the Committee of Sponsoring Organizations of the Treadway Commission (COSO) and the WBCSD included a telling comparison of the results of surveys conducted by the World Economic Forum (WEF) that showed that the prevalence of risks related to ESG steadily increased from 2008 to 2018 while the more traditional economic, geopolitical and technological risks became less dominant.[4] For example, in 2008 only one societal-related risk (pandemics) was reported to be among the top five risks in terms of impact in that year's "Global Risks Report"; however, by 2018 four of the top five risks in the report were either environmental- or social-related: extreme weather events, water crises, natural disasters and failure of climate change mitigation and adaptation.[5] Apart from the WEF survey, news reports have made it clear that companies all around the work have been suffering severe, and sometimes enterprise-ending, adverse financial and/ or reputational impacts from events commonly placed under the umbrella of environmental and social responsibility including product safety recalls, worker fatalities, the discovery of illegal child labor in their supply chains, polluting and delays in the delivery of materials due to climate-related disasters suffered by suppliers.

For COSO and the WBCSD all of this was clear evidence that companies needed to make fundamental changes in their ERM strategies and systems to ensure that they were effectively expanded to include ESG-related risks. From their perspective this means companies must identify and prioritize a new set of risks and build them into their ERM strategies, processes and practice and also realize that there are new opportunities associated with dealing with these risks that can create real value for their investors and other stakeholders. COSO has defined ERM broadly as "the culture, capabilities and practices integrated into strategy and execution that organizations rely on to manage risk and in creating, preserving and realizing value". COSO and the WBCSD illustrated their point as follows:[6]

- Environmental issues include energy use and efficiency, climate change impacts and use of ecosystem services. Associated risks include higher-than-average energy costs that cause companies to miss profit targets and greater frequency of extreme weather events that adversely impact operations; however, companies can take advantage of opportunities such as an internal carbon pricing scheme to reduce greenhouse gas emissions and energy costs and using byproducts in waste processes to create new income streams in adjacent industries.
- Social issues include employee engagement, labor conditions in the supply chain and poverty and community impacts. Associated risks include increased costs and missed profit targets due to low engagement and high turnover and challenges with local governments to maintain operating permits due to lack of support for local communities; however, companies that can successfully engage with employees and create a diverse workforce will enjoy greater loyalty among their workers and be able to attract top talent and companies that can provide education to members of the local community can improve their standard of living, build stronger bonds with the community

and strengthen opportunities to sell goods within the community and recruit local workers.

- Governance issues include codes of conduct, accountability and transparency and disclosures. Associated risks include negative company performance due to poor board oversight and reduced access to financing due to limited transparency; however, proactively embracing ESG issues and risks as a focal point of the board's oversight responsibilities will satisfy the new expectations of institutional investors who are demanding that their companies consider ESG-related risks and opportunities as core to their business.

COSO and the WBCSD expressed concern that while companies appear to understand the importance of ESG-related risks, they have been slow to integrate them with traditional risks. For example, they pointed to evidence of significant misalignment between risks deemed material in sustainability reports prepared by companies and the risks that the companies disclosed in their traditional financial and legal reports. Among the possible reasons for this misalignment were the following:[7]

- The challenges of quantifying ESG-related risks in monetary terms due to the fact that they were often long-term risks with uncertain impacts over an unknown time period. The inability to place a "cash value" on these risks makes it difficult for companies to prioritize them and determine the amount of resources that need to be addressed in order to manage and mitigate those risks.
- A lack of knowledge of ESG-related risks and poor communication and collaboration between risk and sustainability professionals, a situation that has often led to ESG-related risks being viewed as separate and less important than traditional strategic, operational and financial risks.
- The lack of a mainstream practice for integrating reporting of ESG-related risks into traditional financial reports and the difficulties of determining which of those risks is sufficiently material to require reporting.

The problems mentioned above are being addressed in a number of ways including organizational structures that embed sustainability throughout the organization, rather than in a separate unit, and continuous improvements to reporting regimes that make it easier for companies to align strategic, operational, financial and ESG-related risks in their disclosures to regulators and other stakeholders. In 2017 COSO released an initial draft of an updated framework for ERM that reflected the evolution of enterprise risk management and the need to integrate ERM with strategy and performance and incorporate ESG-related risks and opportunities. The framework consisted of the following five components and associated principles that included establishing govern-ance for effective risk management, understanding the business context and strategy, identifying, assessing and prioritizing ESG-related risks, responding to ESG-related risks, reviewing and revising ESG-related risks and, finally, communicating and reporting on ESG-related risks. COSO and WBCSD argued that integrating ESG-related risks into their ERM would allow companies to enhance their resilience, develop a common language for articulating risk, improve resource deployment, enhance pursuit of opportunity, realize efficiencies of scale and improve transparency and disclosure to address the expectations of investors.[8]

Charter and Activities of Compliance and Risk Management Committee

The compliance and risk management committee should have a charter that begins with a statement of purposes and goes on to specify the direct responsibilities of the committee with respect to compliance, risk manage-ment and corporate governance in general. The charter should specify the specific duties and powers of the committee and describe the organizational structure of the committee including any criteria that may be established with respect to the skills and experience of the individual members of the committee. As with other board committees, the compliance and risk man-agement committee should have the right to appoint independent counsel and should also be obligated to make regular reports to the full board of directors.[9]

Statement of Purpose

The charter should include a statement of purpose that addresses both compliance and risk management, recognizing that the two areas overlap substantially. From a compliance perspective, the purpose of the committee can be stated to include oversight of the company's implementation of compliance programs, policies and procedures, including the company's code of conduct, that are designed to respond to the various compli-ance and regulatory risks facing the company; and assisting the board of directors and the other committees of the board, notably the audit and governance committees, in fulfilling their oversight responsibilities for the company's compliance and ethics programs, policies and procedures. When defining compliance, the focus should not only be on relevant laws and regulations but also any voluntary standards that the board has agreed should be adhered to with respect to the day-to-day conduct of the company's operations and other activities. A Global Compact pub-lication recommended that the purpose statement of a risk management committee should include ensuring that the risks and opportunities arising from current and emerging corporate sustainability trends are included and addressed in the company's enterprise risk management program and that the board is informed of material issues relating to current and emerging economic, social and environmental trends.[10]

Composition, Meetings and Procedures

The compliance and risk management committee charter should address composition, frequency of meetings, powers and authority of the committee and other procedures. In general, the same "independence" requirements that apply to audit, governance and compensation committees are also imposed on the members of this committee and it is important that the members of the committee be generally familiar with compliance and ERM issues applicable to the company's specific line of business and operational activities. It is recommended that at least one of the members of the committee have deep experience and technical skills with respect to risk assessment and management, comparable to the qualifications of a financial expert on the audit committee. Given the scope of the mandate of the committee, including the need to regularly receive and review reports from both the chief compliance officer (CCO) and the chief risk officer (CRO), members should expect that meetings will occur frequently and that additional time will need to be invested in interviews and site visits as part of the general oversight of compliance and risk matters.

Scope of Duties and Responsibilities

It is common practice to break out the description of the scope of duties and responsibilities in the committee charter into compliance and risk management. With respect to compliance matters, the compliance and risk management committee should be charged with overseeing the company's activities in the area of compliance that may impact the company's business operations or public image, in light of applicable government and industry standards, as well as legal and business trends and public policy issues.[11] The mandate of the committee can be quite extensive, especially for companies operating in highly regulated industries and markets, and generally includes establishing, in conjunction with the senior management of the company, programs regarding operational and legal compliance and sound business ethics for the company; overseeing the company's relationships with its principal regulatory authorities; reviewing matters relating to the education, training and communications to ensure the company's compliance and ethics policies and procedures are properly disseminated, understood and followed; and monitoring and reviewing the company's activities to ensure that legal requirements and high standards of business and personal ethics are communicated within the company and are being met by the company, its officers and employees and the company's business partners.

The committee should begin its work by assessing the relevant guidelines and procedures relating to legal compliance and ethics. The committee should oversee the development, issuance, distribution and review of such guidelines and procedures and ensure that they meet the requirements of the company's principal regulatory authorities. Once the compliance guidelines and procedures have been approved by the board of directors and senior management, the committee should spend a substantial amount of time and resources on monitoring and assessing implementation of the guidelines and procedures by company management. For example, the committee should make sure that the CCO has direct access to senior management and that sufficient funding, resources and staff have been allocated to the CCO in order for him or her to fully perform the responsibilities of the position; and that the company's code of conduct and written compliance policies and procedures that guide the company and the conduct of its staff in day-to-day operations are being communicated and followed and that relevant education and training for the board and all affected staff and the company's agents on compliance and ethics issues is available. The committee should also be sure that appropriate mechanisms for staff to seek guidance and to report concerns have been launched and are being utilized. This includes clear channels of communication through which employees may seek advice on application of the company's compliance guidelines and report potential compliance violations (e.g., written processes and/or toll-free telephone lines).

The committee should also oversee and receive periodic reports regarding investigations of compliance violations reported to the CCO and ensure that each of the company's business units have processes in place for receiving and investigating reports of compliance violations and advising the CCO of such reports. When necessary, the committee should be involved in investigating alleged misconduct, particularly significant cases of employee conflict of interest, fraud or misconduct, and should proactively promote and enforce standards through incentive and disciplinary actions; however, as a general matter the committee should not plan or conduct specific audits or investigations as those activities are the responsibilities of management. In the event that the company becomes involved in, or is threatened with, litigation or regulatory proceedings bearing on compliance matters the committee should receive regular reports and proactively monitor the company's response to court proceedings and/or audits or examinations by governmental or other regulatory agencies.

As for risk management, Deloitte suggested that the committee should be concerned with overseeing the company's risk exposures and risk management infrastructure; addressing risk and strategy simultaneously, including consideration of risk appetite, and advising the entire board on risk management strategy; monitoring risks; and overseeing and supporting the efforts of the CRO, the company's management risk committee and other groups within the organization formed to monitor risks and implement risk programs.[12] Deloitte noted that it was important to determine how the risk committee will stay informed on developments in risks so it can evolve in its response to them and suggested that such committees develop procedures to ensure that members stay abreast of leading practices as risks evolve and understand the new risks associated with new businesses and locations and how changes in regulations increase or decrease risk. The committee should also benchmark risk governance practices of peers, remain current on risk-related disclosure requirements and conduct annual evaluations of committee performance.

A Global Compact publication recommended that the duties and responsibilities of committees overseeing risk management include:[13]

- Ensuring that sustainability impacts, trends, risks and opportunities are considered in business continuity and disaster recovery plans
- Considering the impact of sustainability trends, risks and opportunities on the company's business, including the impacts on its supply chain, customers, business partners, operating context and overall industry in the short, medium and long-term
- Understanding the opportunities by which sustainability investments can mitigate or influence corporate risks, such as reputation, regulatory, physical, market, strategic, legal, operating risks
- Ensuring sustainability risk management findings are factored into corporate strategy development

Reporting has become an increasingly important aspect of ERM as companies have been pushed to expand the frequency and depth of their disclosures regarding sustainability and governance topics. The compliance and risk management committee should be charged with understanding and approving management's definition of the compliance- and risk-related reports that the committee should receive and it should be prepared to respond to such reports in order to reinforce the importance that the committee places on the reports and their content. The committee members should also be active participants in the review and approval of disclosures in the company's financial statements and other public statements relating to compliance and risks including disclosures by the entire board in the company's public statements regarding the steps that the board and the committee have taken to ensure that the company's compliance programs, compliance audits, risk assessments, responses and interventions have been effective.

Evaluation of Committee Performance

The committee should conduct an annual evaluation of its performance and effectiveness, which may be a self-evaluation or an evaluation employing such other resources or procedures as the committee may deem appropriate. The committee should also review and reassess its charter on a periodic basis, as well as the charters of any management committees created to oversee compliance and/or risk management, and submit any recommended changes to the board for its consideration. Companies will find that there are a number of outside consultants available to assist in evaluating their compliance and ERM programs and performance and make recommendations regarding changes to management processes. In conducting the evaluation, the committee should focus on ensuring that the committee has been kept aware of the significant compliance and risk-related issues that are relevant to the company's business and the industries in which the company operates; the company has an adequate formal framework for conducting its oversight of compliance and ERM activities; and the board regularly reviews progress on the company's performance with respect to compliance and ERM goals, objectives and targets. The committee's evaluation process should be coordinated with similar reviews undertaken by the audit and EH&S committees of the board.

Notes

1 USSG §§ 8A1.1 et seq.
2 G. Goldberg and M. McNamara, *Effective Enterprise Risk Management and Crisis Management: Roles and Responsibilities of the Board and Management* (August 20, 2012), available at www.dentons.com/en/insights/alerts/2012/august/20/effective-enterprise-risk-management-and-crisis-management.
3 Id.
4 *Enterprise Risk Management: Applying Enterprise Risk Management to Environmental, Social and Governance-Related Risks* (Committee of Sponsoring Organizations of the Treadway Commission and the World Business Council for Sustainable Development, Preliminary Draft published February 2018). COSO has been a recognized leader in the development of enterprise risk management frameworks that companies can use to implement effective ERM systems.
5 The two main technological risks in terms of likelihood were cyberattacks and data fraud or theft, each of which comes with substantial reputational and financial risk to companies particularly when the incident involves compromise of consumer information.
6 *Enterprise Risk Management: Applying Enterprise Risk Management to Environmental, Social and Governance-Related Risks* (Committee of Sponsoring Organizations of the Treadway Commission and the World Business Council for Sustainable Development, Preliminary Draft published February 2018), 4.
7 Id. at 7.
8 Id. at 12–13.
9 For examples of compliance and risk management committee charters and additional commentary on preparation of such charters, see "Board Committee Charters" in the management tools available as part of "Governance: A Library of Resources for Sustainable Entrepreneurs" prepared and distributed by the Sustainable Entrepreneurship Project (www.seproject.org).

10 The Essential Role of the Corporate Secretary to Enhance Board Sustainability Oversight: A Best Practices Guide (United Nations Global Compact, September 2016).

11 www.amgen.com/about/how-we-operate/corporate-governance/corporate-responsibility-and-compliance-committee/.

12 www.deloitte.com/view/en_US/us/Services/additional-services/governance-risk-management/67caded005014310VgnVCM3000001c56f00aRCRD.htm.

13 *The Essential Role of the Corporate Secretary to Enhance Board Sustainability Oversight: A Best Practices Guide* (United Nations Global Compact, September 2016).

10 Disclosure and Reporting Committee

Regulators and corporate governance experts all over the world consider disclosure and transparency to be fundamental conditions for properly functioning securities markets. In the U.S., rules and regulations under the Securities Exchange of 1934, as amended (the Exchange Act), as well as pronouncements by the SEC, mandate that every company that becomes subject to the Exchange Act's periodic disclosure requirements (such companies are generally referred to as a "reporting company" and/or "public company") will be expected to prepare annual reports; quarterly reports; current reports and annual reports to shareholders. Companies that have become subject to the disclosure rules must also comply with the Exchange Act's disclosure requirements relating to a wide range of other corporate governance activities including solicitation of proxies, tender offers and "going private" transactions. In addition, directors, officers and principal shareholders of reporting companies are subject to disclosure requirements relating to their ownership interests and changes in those interests.

The Exchange Act also imposes broad obligations on public companies to establish and maintain "disclosure controls and procedures" as well as a system of internal accounting controls. The onus for complying with these obligations falls squarely on the shoulders of the CEO and CFO since each of them is required to evaluate the effectiveness of the disclosure controls and procedures within ninety days prior to the filing of any periodic report required under the Exchange Act and disclose in those reports their conclusions regarding the effectiveness of these controls and procedures. Companies are required to provide investors with internal control reports, as well as related auditor assessment reports, and the CEO and CFO must provide their personal certifications regarding the disclosure controls and procedures and their responsibility for ensuring that such procedures have been established and followed. The CEO and CFO are also required to disclose to the company's outside auditors and to the audit committee all significant defects in the company's internal control procedures. In order to fulfill these obligations, these officers must be actively involved in designing, implementing and monitoring the company's disclosure controls and procedures.

In addition, institutional investors and other stakeholders now expect companies to commit to preparation and dissemination of a sustainability report at determined intervals. The information disclosed in these reports must be prepared in accordance with high quality reporting procedures or as agreed with stakeholders receiving this information and the reports should clearly explain how the performance of the company relates to its corporate social responsibility and corporate governance (CSR/CG) objectives, targets and indicators; provide a comparison of these over time and across organizations; credibly address issues of concern to stakeholders; include information about the performance of the organization measured against its CSR/CG objectives, targets and indicators; describe responsibilities and activities of the various board-level committees overseeing sustainability-related matters; and present a balanced and reasonable assessment of the contribution of the company to sustainable development.[1] One of the fundamental principles of CSR/CG is more transparency by companies with respect to their operational activities and their actual and potential impact on stakeholders beyond investors. As such, it is important for the board to recognize the importance of disclosure and reporting by ensuring that sufficient resources are assigned to understanding and complying with mandatory reporting requirements and creating effective sustainability reports that comply with the emerging guidelines such as those developed by the GRI. In particular, appropriate funding and support needs to be provided for the more comprehensive internal reporting processes required for CSR/CG analysis and reporting.

The disclosure and control requirements associated with public company status can become quite burdensome to the company; however, the ability to access the public capital markets carries with it the responsibility to adhere to the guidelines of the SEC and the stock exchanges with respect to disclosure and protection of stakeholder rights. Responsibility for disclosure processes and internal controls within public companies is vested with a variety of individuals and organizational bodies, including the CEO, CFO and other senior managers; the board of directors as a whole and the audit committee in particular; other specialized committees created by the board of directors, particularly disclosure and reporting committees; the head of the company's internal audit or controls function and that person's internal audit team; other designated managers, including a disclosure controls monitor; and the company's outside auditors. Coordination of the efforts and activities of all of these persons and parties is a demanding task and the costs of compliance for public companies have appreciated significantly. Not only has the level of risk for senior managers increased due to the certification requirements, there is also ongoing uncertainty since the SEC is continuously gathering information regarding the impact of the disclosure requirements, and modifying and expanding those requirements, and standards of "best practices" are slow to emerge.

Sustainability Reporting and Auditing

In order to know whether or not the CSR initiative and its related commitments are actually improving the company's performance it is necessary to have in place procedures for reporting and verification, each of which are important tools for measuring change and communicating those changes to the company's stakeholders. Hohnen and Potts described reporting as "communicating with stakeholders about a firm's economic, environmental and social management and performance" and verification, which is often referred to as "assurance", as a form of measurement that involves on-site inspections and review of management systems to determine levels of conformity to particular criteria set out in codes and standards to which the company may have agreed to adhere.[2]

One basic reason for reporting and verification is to make sure that the CSR initiative is properly managed and that persons involved understand they will be accountable for their actions. Other good reasons for reporting and verification include giving interested parties the information they need in order to make decisions about purchasing the company's products and/or investing in the company (the level of funding from investors focusing their interest on ethical businesses is continuously increasing) or otherwise supporting the company's community activities; collecting information that can be used to make changes and improvements to the company's CSR strategy and commitments; improving internal operations; managing and reducing risks; and strengthening relationships with stakeholders. Libit and Freier argued that CSR reporting provides companies with an opportunity to communicate their CSR efforts to the company's stakeholders, discuss certain successes and challenges with respect to the company on a wide array of CSR issues, demonstrate transparency which can ultimately help to improve the company's reputation with certain stakeholders, provide existing and potential investors with CSR information to assist in analyzing investment decisions and improve the effectiveness of ongoing shareholder relations campaigns such that activist shareholders are deterred from submitting CSR-related shareholder proposals or pursuing or threatening litigation.[3] However, in order to achieve the greatest benefits from reporting and verification companies need to carry out those activities in a rigorous and professional manner using tools and standards that are widely recognized and accepted among those interested in the results.

While CSR-related reporting is not yet specifically required for companies with shares listed on U.S. exchanges, more than half of the companies in the S&P 500 have voluntarily decided to report and disclose CSR information[4] and so-called sustainability reporting is well on its way to becoming an expected standard practice that must be added to the oversight agenda of the entire board and the disclosure and reporting committee. The committee will need to not only understand emerging voluntary reporting standards, such as those developed by the GRI, but also monitor developments in other jurisdictions, such as the European Union and countries in Asia, where regulators have been much quicker to implement formal requirements relating to CSR reporting that may ultimately become the foundation for expanded regulations in the U.S.[5]

The scope of the company's reporting and verification efforts will depend on various factors including the size of the company, the focus of its CSR commitments and the financial and human resources available for investment in those activities. When establishing plans for reporting and verification it is useful to obtain and review copies of reports that have been done and published by comparable companies. Reports of larger companies are generally available on their corporate websites and extensive archives of past CSR-focused reports can be accessed through various online platforms such as CorporateRegister.com, a widely recognized global online directory of corporate responsibility reports, and Sustainability-Reports.com, an international portal for sustainability reporting with news and examples of annual reports with non-financial (sustainability) information. It is also important to have a good working understanding of well-known reporting and verification initiatives such as the GRI Standards; the AccountAbility AA1000 series; the United Nations Global Compact; and the International Auditing and Assurance Standards Board ISAE 3000 standard. Country-specific information is also available through professional organizations such as the Canadian Chartered Professional Accountants, which has published an extensive report on sustainability reporting in Canada.

Global Reporting Initiative Standards

The GRI (www.globalreporting.org) is a multi-stakeholder developed international independent organization that helps businesses, governments and other organizations understand and communicate the impact of business on critical sustainability issues such as climate change, human rights, corruption and many others. GRI has pioneered sustainability reporting since the late 1990s, transforming it from a niche practice to one now adopted by a growing majority of organizations. The GRI Standards are the world's most widely used standards on sustainability reporting and disclosure and available for use by public agencies, firms and other organizations wishing to understand and communicate aspects of their economic, environmental and social performance. The latest version of the GRI Standards were published, following extensive consultation, in October 2016 and formally went into effect for reports and other materials published on or after July 1, 2018. The GRI Standards are divided into four series:[6]

100 Series: The 100 Series includes three universal Standards:

- GRI 101: Foundation is the starting point for using the set of GRI Standards. GRI 101 sets out the Reporting Principles for defining report content and quality. It includes the requirements for preparing a sustainability report in accordance with the GRI Standards, and describes how the GRI Standards can be used and referenced. GRI 101 also includes the specific claims that are required for organizations preparing a sustainability report in accordance with the Standards, and for those using selected GRI Standards to report specific information.
- GRI 102: General Disclosures provide guidance on reporting contextual information about an organization and its sustainability reporting practices. This includes information about an organization's profile, strategy, ethics and integrity, governance, stakeholder engagement practices, and reporting process.
- GRI 103: Management Approach is used to report information about how an organization manages a material topic. It is designed to be used for each material topic in a sustainability report, including those covered by the topic-specific GRI Standards (Series 200, 300 and 400) and other material topics.

Topic-specific Standards: The GRI Standards include three series of topic-specific standards: the 200 Series for economic topics; the 300 Series for environmental topics and the 400 Series for social topics. These topic-specific standards can be used by organizations to report information on their impacts relating to a wide range of economic, environmental and social topics (e.g., indirect economic impacts, water or employment).[7]

International Integrated Reporting Framework

The IIRC (www.integratedreporting.org), which was founded in August 2010, released its International Integrated Reporting Framework in December 2013 as a guide that companies could use to describe how their governance structure creates value in the short, medium and long term; supports decision making that takes into account risks and includes mechanisms for addressing ethical issues; exceeds legal requirements; and ensures that the culture, ethics and values of the company are reflected in its use of and effects on the company's "capitals" (described to include financial, manufactured, intellectual, human, social and relationship, and natural (i.e., the environment and natural resources) forms of value) and stakeholder relationships.[8] Guiding principles for preparation of integrated reports include strategic focus and future orientation, connectivity of information, stakeholder relationships, materiality, conciseness, reliability and completeness, and consistency and comparability.[9]

Sustainability Accounting Standards Board

The Sustainability Accounting Standards Board, or SASB (www.sasb. org), publishes the SASB Implementation Guide for Companies that provides the structure and the key considerations for companies seeking to implement sustainability accounting standards within their existing business functions and processes. The Guide helps companies to select sustainability topics; assess the current state of disclosure and management; embed SASB standards into financial reporting and management processes; support disclosure and management with internal control; and present information for disclosure. The SASB's online resource library also includes annual reports on the state of disclosure, industry briefs and standards and guidance on stakeholder engagement. Companies should monitor CSR disclosures by their peers and the SASB library has examples of disclosures made by companies in annual reports filed with the SEC on Form 10-K. Companies can also follow the reporting practices of competitors by reviewing sustainability reports registered with the GRI.

Verification and Independent External Assurance

Verification procedures should be tailored to the company's organizational culture and the specific elements of the company's CSR strategy and commitments; however, it is common for companies to rely on internal audits, industry (i.e., peer) and stakeholder reviews and professional third party audits. Verification procedures should be established before a specific CSR initiative is undertaken and should be included in the business case for the initiative. While auditing of financial statements by independent outside auditors has long been the norm for listed companies in the U.S. and elsewhere, independent external assurance of sustainability information and reports is still largely voluntary; however, regulators and exchanges generally encourage assurance and including a discussion of steps taken with respect to assurance in the sustainability report itself.

In general, the financial aspects of any sustainability report will be based on the same externally audited financial statements included in the company's traditional annual report. With respect to EH&S matters, companies may engage private quality assurance firms to conduct limited assurances on data relating to, for example, air and water emissions, carbon dioxide generation, recycling/reuse and lost time injury rates. The leading international standard for assuring sustainability reports is ISAE 3000 (Assurance Engagement Other than Audits or Reviews of Historical Financial Information) developed by the International Auditing and Assurance Board, an independent standard-setting board of the International Federation of Accountants. When external assurance is not available or feasible, companies may conduct assurance through internal groups that are organizationally independent of the business units they are reviewing and are specialists in the area with skills necessary to validate and certify operations to various quality, environmental, six sigma and safety standards (e.g., ISO 9000, ISO 14001 and OHSAS 18001).

Role of Audit and Disclosure and Reporting Committees

As discussed above, the SEC has granted public company audit committees substantial authority and responsibility with respect to compliance with the disclosure process. Accordingly, the audit committee should always be a central player in the preparation and review of reports and other disclosure documents, as well as the certifications that must be given by the senior managers (i.e., the CEO and CFO). In most instances, boards do not create separate disclosure and reporting committees and provide for all disclosure and reporting matters to be overseen by the audit committee alone. In those situations, the audit committee itself may create a subcommittee that focuses on disclosure controls and preparation of required and voluntary reports. For the sake of separating out disclosure and reporting from all the other issues that an audit committee must handle, the discussion below pertains to any board-level body specializing in disclosure and reporting (referred to generally as the disclosure and reporting committee), be it a subcommittee of the audit committee or a standalone board committee.[10]

While disclosure and reporting committee members will normally not be included on the internal disclosure committee described above, the controls and procedures should always allow sufficient time for the committee to receive and review each report or other document prior to filing. In general, it is recommended that the disclosure and reporting committee be brought into the process after the internal disclosure committee and the CEO and CFO have completed a final draft of the report or other document and the CEO and CFO are prepared to make the certifications required by law. At that time, the CEO and CFO should present the report or other document to the disclosure and reporting committee and also provide the committee with an oral report that addresses the following issues:

*   The CEO and CFO should confirm that the report or other document was prepared in accordance with the company's written disclosure controls and procedures. The executives should take the opportunity to give committee members a description and explanation of the design and operation of the controls. This should be done regularly, even if a full presentation has been made at prior meetings.
*   The CEO and CFO should provide a description of the steps that they took in order to evaluate the effectiveness of the disclosure controls and procedures, as well as the company's internal controls. In particular, emphasis should be placed on steps taken to identify any

significant deficiencies in the control and any incidences of fraud by employees playing an important role in the disclosure process.

- The committee should also be advised of any significant changes in the internal control system, especially corrective actions that may have been taken in order to address any significant deficiencies uncovered during the evaluation process.
- The CEO and CFO should discuss any material changes that may have been made to the report or other document during the drafting and certification review process. The discussion should focus on how the need to make the change reflects on the efficacy of the company's disclosure controls, and compare the changed disclosure to information provided in prior filings.
- The CEO and CFO should discuss the content and impact of any SEC comments on the particular report or document, as well as the status of any pending or anticipated SEC inquiry relating to the completeness of disclosures made by the company.

As part of their efforts to demonstrate compliance with corporate governance principles to their investors, disclosure and reporting committees should adopt and publish various policies and procedures relating to their disclosure processes and internal controls. For example, a policy statement on disclosure processes and procedures may describe the disclosure process used by the company, including the creation of an internal disclosure committee and appointment of a disclosure controls monitor, and a detailed description taken to insure that disclosure documents are complete and accurate. A statement of policies and procedures regarding internal controls and risk management may be used to describe the principal activities of the company's internal controls or audit function including risk assessment, development of control strategies, implementation of monitoring procedures, and communication of information to senior management, the disclosure and reporting committee and the entire board of directors.

The board-level group responsible for disclosure and reporting matters, be it the audit committee, a subcommittee of the audit committee or a standalone disclosure and reporting committee, should have a set of procedures and formal duties and responsibilities as terms of reference for its activities, generally in the form of a charter. The purpose statement in the charter for a disclosure and reporting committee should include a reference to oversight of management activities in preparing regulatory filings and communications to stakeholders and implementing disclosure controls and procedures which will be in effect to collect, analyze and disseminate the information necessary for the company to meet its financial and sustainability reporting obligations and commitments. The charter should explain how the disclosure and reporting committee fits within the organizational structure of the other board committees, particularly the audit, compensation and CSR committees, and the allocation of duties and responsibilities between the board-level committee and any internal disclosure committee created by the CEO and CFO. Issues with respect to boundaries can easily be addressed by ensuring the disclosure and reporting committee includes members of the audit, compensation and CSR committees and having representatives of all four committees meet as a single group at regular intervals.

Other factors to consider when creating a board-level disclosure and reporting committee are the size of the committee and the diversity of the membership. Studies have shown that companies that are willing and able to implement broader, more objective and more comparable information practices are able to generate added value and an enhanced social and environmental impact.[11] One way to ensure that information processes are robust, integrated and sufficient to generate the information necessary to prepare reports that meet the needs of all stakeholders of the company, not just financial-based disclosures to shareholders, is populating the disclosure and reporting committee with members who bring a diverse set of perspectives to the process and truly understand what is material to current and prospective employees, customers, regulators and members of the communities in which the company operates.[12] As alluded to above, stakeholder engagement is foundational to sustainability reporting and committee members should be versed in engagement techniques and prepared to participate directly in communications with stakeholders to identify their key interests.

A list of duties and responsibilities for the disclosure and reporting committee would likely be extensive and include the following tasks:

- Review and, as necessary, help revise the company's controls and other procedures (Disclosure Controls and Procedures) to ensure that information required by the company to be disclosed to the SEC and other regulatory bodies, and other written information that the company will disclose to the public, is recorded, processed, summarized and reported accurately and on a timely basis, and such information is accumulated and communicated to management, including the CEO and CFO, as appropriate to allow timely decisions regarding required disclosures
- Understand and review the processes adopted by management with respect to documenting, and monitoring the integrity and evaluating the effectiveness of, the Disclosure Controls and Procedures including the establishment and management of an internal disclosure committee
- Review (i) the company's annual, quarterly and periodic reports; proxy statements, material registration statements, and any other

information filed with the SEC and other regulatory bodies (Reports), (ii) press releases containing financial information, earnings guidance, forward-looking statements, information about material transactions, or other information material to the company's stakeholders, (iii) correspondence broadly disseminated to stakeholders and (iv) other relevant communications or presentations (Disclosure Statements)

- Prepare and recommend to the board of directors a policy regarding disclosures to be adopted by the board with respect to Disclosure Controls and Procedures and reviews of Reports and Disclosure Statements
- Discuss information relative to the committee's responsibilities and proceedings, including (i) the preparation of the Disclosure Statements and (ii) the evaluation of the effectiveness of the Disclosure Controls and Procedures
- Understand the processes used by management to identify what constitutes a significant deficiency and material weakness in the design or operation of internal control and review actions proposed to be taken by management with respect to disclosure and remediation of significant control deficiencies
- Assume oversight responsibility for all primary components of the sustainability reporting process including identification of material sustainability factors, establishment of policies in relation to the identified factors, establishment of performance targets for each identified factor, selection of a globally recognized sustainability reporting framework and establishment of assurance procedures for sustainability reporting
- Receive and review on a continuous basis reports from the CEO and the company's CSO on (i) sustainability trends and impacts on the company's operations, financial results and stakeholders and (ii) the company's positions on and actions taken relating to relevant sustainability issues and how such positions and actions have affected or may affect stakeholders.
- Ensure that information necessary for the preparation of sustainability reports is collected within the framework of the company's overall disclosure controls and practices
- Regularly meet with the members of the team selected to assume responsibility for the preparation of the sustainability report, which should include representatives of relevant departments such as investor relations, governmental/regulatory relations, community relations, legal compliance and human resources
- Ensure that clear processes and standard methods have been established to ensure that data necessary for the preparation of the sustainability report is collected and analyzed and that senior management understands the importance of balanced sustainability reporting

- Receive regular reports on activities relating to stakeholder engagement including meetings and other dialogues with investors, employee representatives, community members and supply chain partners
- Regularly meet with members of other board-level committees responsible for areas such as auditing, governance, compliance, risk management, CSR, environmental and health and safety to ensure coordination of data collection and reporting activities
- Regularly review the steps taken by management with respect to external assessment of information included in sustainability reports and external certification of sustainability-related operations
- Prepare and submit to the full board of directors for review and approval a board statement on the board having considered sustainability issues as part of its strategic formulation, determined the material sustainability factors and overseen the management and monitoring of the material sustainability factors
- Ensure that board members, senior management and relevant employees throughout the organization receive training on sustainability report techniques and trends
- Oversee presentation of sustainability-related information on the company's website

While the scope of the activities and responsibilities of the disclosure and reporting committee is obviously quite extensive, the frequency of committee meetings will depend in large part on the ability of the committee and management to establish and maintain disclosure controls that effectively identify major issues that warrant attention at the board level. The committee should meet no less frequently than quarterly and may designate a sub-group of the committee to be available for consultation and review with respect to disclosures outside of the periodic reporting schedule. All regular meetings should include presentations by the CEO, CFO and any designated leader of the internal disclosure committee and the committee should also meet regularly with representatives of the company's independent auditors and the internal audit group. Disclosure and reporting committees should consider engaging outside consultants, typically attorneys and accountants who have worked for the SEC and other regulatory bodies, to conduct an independent review of proposed disclosures and access the reaction of regulators to the disclosures once they are filed. A similar independent review should be conducted of disclosures in sustainability reports to gauge whether the information reasonably addresses the expectations of stakeholder groups and reflects the communications that occurred during the engagement process. Like other board-level committees, the disclosure and reporting committee should conduct an evaluation of its performance and issue a report to the board with recommendations relating to changes to the purposes and duties of the committee.

Notes

1 P. Castka, C. Bamber and J. Sharp, *Implementing Effective Corporate Social Responsibility and Corporate Governance: A Framework* (British Standards Institution and the High Performance Organization Ltd., 2005), 6–8.
2 P. Hohnen (Author) and J. Potts (Editor), *Corporate Social Responsibility: An Implementation Guide for Business* (Winnipeg CAN: International Institute for Sustainable Development, 2007), 67.
3 B. Libit and T. Freier, *The Corporate Social Responsibility Report and Effective Stakeholder Engagement* (Chapman and Cutler LLP, 2013), available at https://corpgov.law.harvard.edu/2013/12/28/the-corporate-social-responsibility-report-and-effective-stakeholder-engagement/ (accessed May 12, 2020).
4 As cited in H. Gregory, *Corporate Social Responsibility*, available at www.practicallaw.com (April 2014).
5 A powerful and useful resource for monitoring actions regarding sustainability reporting among stock exchanges around the world is the United Nations' Sustainable Stock Exchanges (SSE) initiative (www.sseinitiative.org/), which is a peer-to-peer learning platform for exploring how exchanges, in collaboration with investors, regulators and companies, can enhance corporate transparency–and ultimately performance–on ESG (environmental, social and corporate governance) issues and encourage sustainable investment.
6 GRI 101: Foundation 2016 (Amsterdam: Stichting Global Reporting Initiative, 2016), 4.
7 For further discussion of sustainability reporting using the GRI Standards, see A. Gutterman, *Sustainability Reporting and Auditing* (New York: Business Experts Press, 2020).
8 P. DeSimone, *Board Oversight of Sustainability Issues: A Study of the S&P 500* (IRRC Institute, March 2014), 7.
9 *The International <IR> Framework* (London: The International Integrated Reporting Council, December 2013), 5.
10 For discussion of the duties and responsibilities of the audit committee, see Chapter 5 (Audit Committee) in this volume.
11 See, e.g., L. Rodríguez-Ariza, I. García-Sánchez and J. Frías-Aceituno, *The Role of the Board in Achieving Integrated Financial and Sustainability Reporting* (examined 568 non-financial firms from 15 countries, including firms from Anglo-Saxon, Germanic and Latin models of corporation governance, for the period 2008–2010).
12 For discussions of empirical studies of the impact of board composition on sustainability reporting, see D. Dienes and P. Velte, "The Impact of Supervisory Board Composition on CSR Reporting: Evidence from the German Two-Tier System", *Sustainability*, 8 (2016), 63 (gender diversity among the membership of German supervisory boards found to have a positive impact on CSR disclosure intensity) and Z. Mahmood, R. Kouser, W. Ali, Z. Ahmad and T. Salman, "Does Corporate Governance Affect Sustainability Disclosure?: A Mixed Methods Study", *Sustainability*, 10 (2018), 207 (using data collected from 100 companies listed on the Pakistan Stock Exchange for the period ranging from 2012 to 2015 to provide support for the proposition that a large board size consisting of a female director and a CSR committee is better able to check and control management decisions regarding sustainability issues and results in better sustainability disclosure).

11 Internal Governance Instruments

Corporate governance involves a set of relationships between a company's management, its board, its shareholders and other stakeholders and effective governance requires a structure through which the objectives of the company are set, the means of attaining those objectives and monitoring performance are determined, and the company and its people are held accountable.[1] Since the elements of corporate governance include ethics, risk management, compliance and administration, companies must establish and maintain the appropriate "control environment" in order for their corporate governance procedures to be effective. The term refers to the mindset and philosophy that drives decision making and attitudes throughout the organization. The environment must be established at the top of the organization hierarchy, beginning with the board of directors and its various committees, particularly the audit committee, as well as with senior management. Then it needs to be reinforced throughout the company by employee training and the values that are rewarded with respect to the behavior and performance of employees.

One of the first steps in establishing the appropriate control environment is the adoption and dissemination of corporate governance instruments in the form of codes, policies and procedures. Written codes, policies and procedures are not only important in making sure that the corporate governance program is properly implemented and monitored, they can also serve as a useful public relations tool. The content of certain governance-related codes and policies is often driven by regulatory requirements. For example, the Sarbanes-Oxley Act of 2002 (SOX) provided that periodic reports filed with the SEC must disclose whether or not (and if not, why not) the company has adopted a code of ethics for senior financial officers (i.e., CFO and principal accounting officer or controller).[2] Both the NYSE and Nasdaq have embraced the requirements of SOX in their listing standards and have actually expanded the scope of coverage beyond senior executive and financial officers to include all directors, officers and employees.[3] In addition, many companies are now adopting corporate governance guidelines, which are actually required for NYSE-listed companies.[4] Finally, companies typically also adopt an extensive code of business conduct that addresses many aspects of the day-to-day activities of the company and each of its employees and supplement the code with additional corporate policies relating to specific compliance areas.

Principles of Corporate Governance

The first step in establishing a portfolio of internal governance instruments is the preparation, approval and implementation of foundation principles of corporate governance as determined by the board of directors in line with the requirements of statutes, regulatory guidance and, in the case of public companies, listing guidelines. Regardless of whether the board has adopted formal corporate governance principles, directors, when discharging their duties as a director, are expected to act in good faith and in a manner the director reasonably believes to be in the best interests of the corporation.[5] In addition, board members, when becoming informed in connection with their decision-making function or devoting attention to their oversight function, must discharge their duties with the care that a person in a like position would reasonably believe appropriate under similar circumstances (i.e., the so-called "duty of care").[6] Corporate governance principles are designed to lay out a series of basic rules that the entire board, as well as individual directors, can refer to as a guide for fulfilling their fiduciary duties.

Corporate governance principles should be drafted to conform to the corporate law of the state in which the corporation is incorporated and organized, since this is the primary source of the law relating to the duties and rights of corporate directors and officers. Even public companies need to abide by state law regulations relating to such things as number of directors; qualifications of directors; election of directors; terms of directors; shareholders' rights to remove directors; and directors' meetings and actions. A number of states, notably California, Delaware and New York, have periodically amended their corporation laws to accommodate the changing needs of public companies that are incorporated in their states. For example, state laws now accommodate the common practice of staggered terms for directors and have continuously updated their rules and regulations relating to indemnification of directors and officers. In addition, state law is the primary source of the essential duties of directors and officers to the corporation and its shareholders, notably the duty of care and duty of loyalty in the course of discharging their obligations. In fact, the reporting obligations imposed under revisions to federal law specifically refer to potential violations of fiduciary duty by directors and officers, as well as violations of federal securities laws. In addition to their duties and potential liabilities under state corporation laws, corporate directors and officers of public companies are subject to substantial potential liabilities for violations of federal securities laws. Among the areas of greatest concern is the possibility of liability for violations of insider trading rules and restrictions and for misrepresentations in registration statements filed under the Securities Act.

Obviously companies should take into account any specific laws, regulations and listing standards when drafting their corporate governance guidelines and the format for presenting the information will vary depending on the preferences of the drafting group. In general, however, the following topics should be covered:[7]

- *Composition and Organization of Board of Directors:* Size of the board; membership qualifications; selection procedures; independence requirements; term limits; retirement age; changes in professional responsibilities; and guidelines for selection of the chairperson of the board.
- *Duties and Responsibilities of Directors:* Adoption of procedures for review of contracts and allocation of signature authority with respect to company contracts; guidelines for the regular assessment of the performance of the board of directors; procedures for evaluation of the performance of the CEO and other members of the senior management team; procedures for succession planning and leadership development; procedures for director involvement in the formulation and evaluation of the company's strategic and operating plans; conditions and procedures relating to interaction of board members with investors, the media and company business partners; and plans for director development including new director orientation and continuing director education.
- *Director Compensation and Related-Party Transactions:* Establishment of compensation policies for directors; procedures for setting compensation, including participation by the nominating and corporate governance committee of the board; requirements as to minimum stock ownership; and procedures for preventing conflicts of interest and approving related-party transactions.
- *Meetings and Committees of the Board of Directors:* Preparation and attendance; frequency and length of meetings; meeting agenda; distribution of meeting materials; executive sessions; attendance of non-directors at meetings; director access to senior management and other information regarding the company and its business activities; director access to independent advisors; number of committees; assignment of board members to committees; committee charters and authority; committee agendas; frequency and length of committee meetings; and executive sessions.

Codes of Conduct and Ethics

The board of directors is responsible for the company's efforts to comply with applicable laws and regulations, as well as any voluntary standards that the company has publicly endorsed and integrated into their internal operational guidelines. The foundation of any compliance program is a code of conduct that sets the basic internal standards to be observed by all directors, officers and employees of the company in order to establish, maintain and strengthen the business ethics and compliance systems throughout the company. The code of conduct is intended to serve as a guide for managers and employees to make good decisions and conduct business ethically. In addition to legal and regulatory compliance standards, the code of conduct will also state the company's intention to engage in ethical business practices with respect to such areas as respect for human rights, safety of products and services, environmental conservation and information disclosure.

When preparing a code of conduct, it is customary to include a description of the legal requirements that apply to the company business and operations; examples of specific types of conduct that will actually or potentially violate those requirements; and a description of the methods that the company intends to use to ensure that the code is followed, including specific penalties that the company may apply. This information may be included in the code itself, or the drafter may elect to cover the topics in separate appendices such as a summary description of the relevant laws and regulations pertaining to the company's business activities. Beyond specific examples, the code may also include a statement of certain core company values and principles which may serve as a guide for employees to select appropriate and lawful behavior in situations that have not been discussed in advance as part of the code.

Since the code of conduct is directed at all employees within the company, it is important to include a description of the rules and guidelines that the company intends to adhere to with regard to workplace activities and relationships. In this area, reference should be made to solid human resources practices, including all the types of things that might lead to a claim against the company under the employment laws. Among other things, the code or policy should discuss company rules relating to unlawful harassment and discrimination, workplace health and safety, substance abuse, conflicts of interest, outside employment and electronic communications.

The code of conduct should also discuss the rules and regulations that are relevant to the day-to-day conduct of business activities with key outside partners of the company, including its customers and suppliers. Each of these partners, as well as the general community, will demand assurances that the company conducts itself in a manner that complies with the law and with commonly accepted standards of business ethics in the relevant industry. Areas of greatest concern include representations and warranties to customers regarding the company's products and services, sound contracting practices, compliance with antitrust and competition laws and protection of confidential information disclosed to the company by its business partners.

In addition, the code of conduct should demonstrate that the company is mindful of its duties and obligations to its shareholders, particularly outside investors not actively involved in the day-to-day activities of the company. In the case of companies subject to SOX, the code of conduct should confirm that adequate internal controls are being maintained and that investors are being provided with full and accurate disclosure of financial and business information on a timely basis. Beyond that, however, investors must be assured that company insiders are not engaged in unlawful trading of the company's securities based on information that has not been disclosed to the marketplace. The code should also demonstrate that the company is taking adequate steps to protect its tangible and intangible assets, including its intellectual property rights.

Finally, the code of conduct should demonstrate recognition of the company's role and obligations within its broader communities. For example, employees should be provided with guidelines relating to participation in political activities. Companies involved in business activities outside of the U.S. must be mindful of local customs and practices, as well as the wide range of laws regulating corrupt practices, boycotts, export controls, formation and operation of joint ventures and immigration. Depending on the type of business, attention may also need to focus on environmental regulation and rules governing transport of hazardous materials and certain types of goods.

The code of conduct should be disseminated to all employees of the company, particularly employees working in foreign countries, with a cover letter from the company's CEO to demonstrate the commitment of senior management to the principles set forth in the code. Employees should also have access to the code on the intranet websites of the individual branches and subsidiaries within the company. In addition, the code should be part of the company's compliance training and education programs and the following procedures should be implemented to demonstrate that the code has been disseminated: each employee should execute and deliver an initial attestation that they have received and reviewed the code (this should occur for all current employees when the code is first distributed; and, thereafter, an initial attestation should be collected from each new employee when he or she joins the company); following their initial attestation, all employees should be required to execute and deliver an annual attestation throughout their employment with the company that confirms their continued understanding of their duties and obligations under the code; and all supervisors responsible for collection of the employee attestations should prepare and sign a report that confirms either that the attestations have been collected or that certain employees identified on the report declined to sign their attestation (obviously, an election by an employee to not sign an attestation should trigger further inquiries by the supervisor and the compliance team).

Board of Directors' Code of Conduct

In addition to the corporate governance principles, directors will often adopt a specific code of business conduct and ethics relating to areas of specific concern to members of the board as they discharge their duties on behalf of the company. Among the issues that are typically addressed in a directors' code of business conduct are the following:

- *Fiduciary Duties:* The directors' code of conduct should explicitly state and reinforce each director's statutory and case law obligation to act in the best interests of, and fulfill their fiduciary obligations to, all of the company's stakeholders, and act in good faith, responsibly, with due care, competence and diligence, without allowing their independent judgment to be subordinated.
- *Conflicts of Interest:* In furtherance of the company's overriding goal to establish fair and honest dealings with customers, coworkers, suppliers, competitors and other business partners, directors are expected to set an example by avoiding conflicts of interest, which are situations in which the private interest or outside economic interests of a director (or a family member of the director) interferes with his or her responsibilities to or judgment on behalf of the company. Conflicted directors are required to notify the leadership of the board as promptly as practicable and refrain from participating in any deliberations and decisions by the board that in any way relates to the matter that gives rise to the conflict of interest. Concerns about conflicts of interest should be broadly construed and directors should avoid even the appearance of a conflict of interest, even if no real issues exist.
- *Corporate Opportunities:* Directors owe a duty to their companies to advance the company's legitimate interests when the opportunity to do so arises and thus are prohibited from taking any business opportunity for themselves (or directing a business opportunity to a third party) if that opportunity is discovered through the use of the company's property, information or position. The only exception to this rule is in situations where the company has already been offered the opportunity and determined that it will not pursue that opportunity. The fundamental principle underlying the rules surrounding business opportunities is that directors may not use their company's property, information or position for personal gain or to engage in competition with the company.
- *Protection of Confidential Information:* Directors, like officers and employees of the company, are under a fiduciary obligation to the

company, both during and after his or her term of office, to maintain the confidentiality of information entrusted to him or her by the company and any other confidential information about the company that comes to him or her, from whatever source, in his or her capacity as a director. Directors are forbidden from disclosing confidential information to any persons or entities outside of the company, except in limited circumstances, and from using the company's confidential information to their personal advantage or to benefit persons or entities outside the company.

- *Protection and Proper Use of Assets:* Consistent with the rules relating to business opportunities and protection of confidential information discussed above, directors have a broader duty to protect the assets, tangible and intangible, of the company and ensure that they are used only for legitimate business purposes and not for the personal benefit or gain of any director (or family member of the director).

- *Inside Information and Securities Trading:* Directors obviously have access to confidential or material nonpublic information regarding the company and value elements of the company's stock that is not available to others who might be trading in the marketplace for the company's stock. Directors are strictly forbidden from engaging in stock transactions with respect to the company's stock while they have knowledge of confidential or material nonpublic information from or about the company, even if they reasonably believe they are not using or relying on that nonpublic information in making their own investment decisions. Insider trading is not only unethical, it is illegal, and public companies typically have extensive rules that directors must follow in order to buy or sell the company's securities.

- *Compliance with Laws, Rules and Regulations; Fair Dealing:* Directors should acknowledge their obligation to comply with all laws, rules and regulations applicable to them as directors of the company and observe the highest ethical standards and act to promote an environment of fairness, integrity and honesty inside the organization and in relationships with other directors and with the company's customers, suppliers and competitors. Simply put, directors have a real obligation to protect and enhance the company's reputational capital.

- *Public Disclosures:* While directors are recognized as leaders and symbols of the company, they should refrain from responding to inquiries from or speaking with the investment community or the news media unless they have received authorization from an authorized company spokesperson, typically someone working with the company's public relations department.

- *Reporting Illegal or Unethical Behavior:* Directors have a duty to communicate any suspected violations of the directors' code of conduct, including any unethical behavior, violation of law or governmental rule or regulation, promptly to the chairperson of the board and/or the chairperson of the board's governance committee, at which point the alleged violations will be investigated by the board (or by a person or persons designated by the board) and appropriate action will be taken in the event it is found that a violation of the code has occurred.

Each director should be required to sign a formal written acknowledgment of the contents of the directors' code of conduct and attest to compliance on an annual basis by delivery of an additional written attestation form. The code should be reviewed regularly and, while provision may be made for amendments and waivers, a waiver should only be granted in limited, special circumstances after disclosure of all facts to, and deliberation by, the entire board or the board's governance committee. When considering whether to grant a waiver, it is important to remember that waivers must be promptly disclosed in accordance with applicable law and the requirements of the exchange on which the company's securities are listed and traded. The governance committee, in furtherance of its role in director development, should provide periodic training on each of the topics covered in the directors' code of conduct.

CEO/CFO Code of Ethics

Each issuer required to file periodic reports with the SEC pursuant to Section 13(a) or 15(d) of the Exchange Act must disclose in its Form 10-K whether (and, if not, why not) it has adopted a written code of ethics for the company's principal executive officer and senior financial officers and must also disclose on Form 8-K (or, under some circumstances, on its website) any substantive changes to or waivers of the code. The definition of "code of ethics" calls for drafting written standards that are reasonably designed to deter wrongdoing and to promote: honest and ethical conduct, including the ethical handling of actual or apparent conflicts of interest between personal and professional relationships; full, fair, accurate, timely and understandable disclosure in reports and documents that an issuer files with, or submits to, the SEC and in other public communications made by the issuer; compliance with applicable governmental laws, rules and regulations; prompt internal reporting of violations of the code of ethics to the individual(s) identified in the code; and accountability for adherence to the code. If adopted, the code of ethics must be made available to the public by one of the three following means: filing it with the SEC as an exhibit to Form 10-K; posting it on the issuer's website and disclosing, in Form 10-K, the website address and the fact that the issuer has posted its code of ethics; or undertaking in Form 10-K to provide to any person without charge, on request, a copy of such code of ethics and explain the manner in which such request may be made.[8]

Ancillary Board Policies

Public companies typically adopt several ancillary board policies to address specific requirements of the exchanges upon which their securities are listed. For example, the Nasdaq listing rules require that a majority of the board of directors must be comprised of "independent directors", as determined using the definition described below, and companies must disclose in their annual proxy (or, if the company does not file a proxy, in its Form 10-K or 20-F) those directors that the board of directors has determined to be independent under the applicable definition.[9] In addition, independent directors must have regularly scheduled meetings at which only independent directors are present ("executive sessions").[10] The Commentary on this requirement notes that regularly scheduled executive sessions encourage and enhance communication among independent directors and that it is contemplated that executive sessions will occur at least twice a year, and perhaps more frequently, in conjunction with regularly scheduled board meetings.[11] NYSE-listed companies must also have a majority of independent directors.[12] The NYSE Listing Manual also provides that in order to empower non-management directors to serve as a more effective check on management, the non-management directors of each listed company must meet at regularly scheduled executive sessions without management.[13]

In order to assist in fulfilling the "independent director" requirements, the board will adopt a policy that includes the definition of "independence" that must be satisfied by prospective directors other than those who are employed by the company. Each company should draft a definition statement that follows the rules promulgated by the securities exchange on which the company's shares are listed and the definition statement should be posted on the company's website for public review and incorporated into the director qualification guidelines discussed below. The entire board of directors should regularly determine, on a formal basis, that its non-employee directors are "independent" within the meaning of the definition. If they wish, directors may incorporate specific thresholds for concepts such as "significant" that are included in the information statement by referencing the "bright-line" standards for disqualification as "independent" including in the requirements adopted by the exchanges.

Independence is just one of the criteria for prospective directors and the board should also adopt guidelines that the nominating or corporate governance committee can follow in evaluating prospective candidates for the board of directors. The guidelines will obviously vary depending on the type of company and its activities; however, emphasis is normally placed on management experience; knowledge and training in various functional areas, such as finance and accounting; and the contribution that the candidate can make with respect to attaining stated goals and objectives relating to the diversity of the board in terms of criteria such as race, ethnicity, age, sex, location, occupation etc.

As companies have embraced sustainability as integral to their long-term strategies and as a means for building and maintaining a strong reputation and brand, directors' qualifications have expanded to include expertise, skills and experience in sustainability-related areas; ability and willingness to represent the long- and short-term interests of not just stockholders, but also all the other stakeholders of the company; awareness of the company's responsibilities to its customers, employees, suppliers, regulatory bodies and the communities in which it operates; willingness to participate in engagement activities with the company's stakeholders and be available to receive and respond to communications from stakeholder representatives; understanding of the environmental and social responsibility challenges confronting the company and willingness to participate in integrating solutions to those challenges in the company's long-term strategy; and understanding of "triple bottom line" disclosure and reporting requirements and the methods used to measure and describe environmental, social and economic performance. The guidelines should also describe the expectations associated with service on the board, including participation in meetings and the willingness to devote sufficient time to review information and communicating with management. These guidelines should be posted on the company's website for public review.

Sustainability-Related Instruments

The instruments described above establish a foundation for all companies striving to develop an effective corporate governance framework. However, the integration of sustainability into corporate governance means that companies must implement additional sustainability-related instruments, as well as updating traditional codes and policies to cover topics and actions related to sustainability and CSR. At a minimum, companies should supplement their corporate governance principles and ethics codes with additional policies on specific topics and issues such as work environment, political contributions, anti-bribery, conflicts of interest and/ or health and safety practices. A supplier code of conduct should also be implemented to provide guidance on overseeing the actions of supply chain partners with respect to key sustainability issues. In addition, a separate statement of sustainability commitments should be developed, approved and disseminated by the board of directors.[14]

Notes

1 www.governanceinstitute.com.au/knowledge-resources/governance-foundations/more-thoughts-on-governance/.
2 Sarbanes-Oxley Act § 406(a), 15 USC § 7264(a).

3 See the provisions of the Rule 5600 Series of the Nasdaq Listing Rules relating to codes of conduct and NYSE Listing Manual § 303A.10.

4 See NYSE Listing Manual § 303A.09.

5 Model Business Corporations Act § 8.30(a).

6 Id. at § 8.30(b).

7 For further details, see NYSE Listing Manual § 303A.08 (procedures relating to contents and disclosure of corporate governance guidelines for NYSE-listed companies). Nasdaq does not have specific requirements with respect to content and adoption of corporate governance guidelines; however, it should be expected that companies subject to Nasdaq listing standards should adopt guidelines on a voluntary basis that address all of the categories of corporate governance regulated by Nasdaq including distribution of annual or interim reports, independent directors, audit and compensation committees, nomination of directors, code of conduct, annual meetings, solicitation of proxies, quorum, conflicts of interest, shareholder approvals and voting rights. Reference should be made to the then-current version of the Corporate Governance Guidelines adopted by Nasdaq's own board of directors for insights into the subjects that Nasdaq listed companies should consider including in their own corporate governance principles.

8 17 CFR § 229.406(c)

9 Nasdaq Listing Rule 5605(b)(1). Nasdaq Listing Rule 5605(a)(2) defines the term "Independent Director" to mean a person other than an Executive Officer (defined as those officers covered in Rule 16a-1(f) under the Exchange Act) or employee of the company or any other individual having a relationship which, in the opinion of the company's board of directors, would interfere with the exercise of independent judgment in carrying out the responsibilities of a director.

10 Nasdaq Listing Rule 5605(b)(2).

11 Nasdaq Listing Rule IM-5605-2.

12 NYSE Listing Manual § 303A.01. The definition of "independent director" for purposes of NYSE differs from the Nasdaq and reference should be made to the specific conditions in NYSE Listing Manual § 303A.02.

13 NYSE Listing Manual § 303A.03.

14 For further discussion of sustainability-related governance instruments, see A. Gutterman, Sustainability Management (New York: Routledge, 2020).

12 Organizing for Sustainability

CSR requires proactive leadership from the top of the organization including engaged oversight by the board of directors.[1] However, while the directors must set and monitor CSR-related commitments and strategies, the day-to-day responsibilities, including continuous interactions with stakeholders, must be assumed by the officers of the company and will require design and implementation of effective internal organizational structures and systems for managing CSR initiatives and programs. This chapter surveys a few of the key issues relating to organizing for sustainability including the roles of the CEO and other sustainability leaders, organizational structures for sustainability activities and sustainability-related management systems.

Role of the CEO in CSR Activities

Surveys, such as one completed by Boyden in 2017 among adults in the U.K., repeatedly confirm that the public strongly believes that the CEO must play an active role in the CSR activities of his or her company and act as a spokesperson for those activities.[2] Participation and engagement by employees throughout the organization is essential for effective human capital management and CSR implementation and the CEO is the only person in a position to communicate and demonstrate the values associated with CSR in a way that will integrate CSR into the corporate culture and the way that employees work on a day-to-day basis. It should be noted that CSR has become a significant driver of employee engagement, particularly among Millennials who are more willing to accept lower wages in exchange for working with a company committed to sustainability, and that the CEO's efforts to engage employees in this area will improve the company's ability to attract and retain talented workers. CEOs must also develop the soft skills necessary to communicate and engage with multiple stakeholders, each of which has different values and attitudes about how society should function and the role that the firm should play. CEOs must be able to engage in civil dialogue, approach the problems and challenges that are raised by stakeholders with an open mind and a focus on identifying and implementing innovative solutions and developing tools that will help measure and demonstrate the effectiveness and value of the company's CSR initiatives.

Selecting the CEO and other members of the executive team, and setting the right performance criteria and incentives with respect to pursuit and achievement of the company's sustainability commitments and targets, is a unique and important responsibility of the board of directors. At the very beginning, during the recruitment process, Global Compact LEAD calls on directors to include in their selection criteria that candidates have the ability to demonstrate solid understanding of the complex sustainability issues that affect the business environment; commit to operate in accordance with the highest social, environmental and ethical standards; and provide a track record of producing excellent financial results with due consideration for the interests and concerns of different stakeholders.[3]

Once candidates for CEO and the other spots on the executive team have been selected, incentives must be put in place in their compensation arrangements that reward long-term performance and that are aligned with the sustainability priorities and targets established by the board. Not only does this impact the decisions that the executive team make but it also sends a strong message to employees and external stakeholders about how sustainability is valued and taken seriously at the top of the organization. Global Compact LEAD suggests that two ways to incentivize good sustainability performance might be linking part of executive pay to stocks, bonds or escrow that are only released after ten or fifteen years and making a portion of the performance-based salary dependent on the realization of the short-term sustainability objectives of a company.[4]

When setting "sustainability objectives" for which performance will be measured and compensation determined, emphasis should be on the specific issues and priorities that are material to the company such as the chosen targets for carbon emissions, health and safety incidents, gender diversity or sales of certain categories of sustainable products.[5] Performance measurement with respect to sustainability indicators can be challenging given the lack of necessary data and the need for some level of discretion to be used when objective information is not easily available. When discretion is used, it is important for it to be verifiable and based on an independent process. Sustainability incentives must also be meaningful in the broader context of the executive's entire compensation package.[6]

Organizational Structures for Sustainability

While sustainability has become an important issue for companies of all sizes, most are still struggling with understanding and implementing "sustainable organizational design principles" in their infrastructures and supply chains.[7] Alignment of organizational design and sustainability should begin with the development of a sustainability strategy and accompanying goals and priorities based on stakeholder engagement and vetted and approved by the board of directors. In order for the sustainability strategy to be effective and successful, it must align with the structure, competencies and culture of the company. Strategies should be based on an overall vision for the company and a set of commitments that serve as the foundation for strategies and tactics and bind all of the business units together to work toward a common purpose. Commitments should be pursued through a combination of corporate policies, sustainability policies and employee initiatives. Companies should embed sustainability into their organizations through cross-functional teams, clear targets and key performance indicators. Experiences of various companies have illustrated that it is important to introduce smaller organizational structures into the mix that facilitate mobilization of local communities to work on issues that will contribute to sustainability in their communities.[8]

Companies that are relatively new to sustainability often begin with a fairly simple "stand-alone" structure based on treating the sustainability program as a separate function like finance, operations or marketing.[9] A high level executive, often given the title "chief sustainability officer" (CSO), will oversee the function and reports directly to the CEO from the same level in the organizational hierarchy as other C-level executives. The job of the CSO is to begin the difficult process of engaging the business units that are overseen by other C-level executives through a structure that might have a vice president of sustainability reporting to the CSO and overseeing operations of the sustainability group and directors who report to the CSO or vice president and are charged with various sustainability-related activities such as communications, philanthropy, procurement strategy and environmental issues. The advantages of this type of structure are that it creates a group that is solely focused on and responsible for initiating and implementing sustainability-related activities and it serves as a magnet for recruiting the specialized skills necessary for sustainable programs to be successful. The structure also provides clear control and coordination of the portfolio of sustainability-related activities and associated budgets. However, a standalone approach has several critical drawbacks: sustainability is not integrated into the rest of the organization; limited buy-in from employees because they are not accountable to the sustainability function; and funding challenges since the function is typically focused on reducing costs as opposed to business development.

Companies often attempt to address and resolve some of the key shortcomings of the standalone structure by designing an "integrated structure" that recognizes and promotes reporting relationships between the sustainability directors, still sitting primarily in the sustainability function, and the business units. Advantages of this approach include enablement of organization-wide integration and the creation of direct ties between the sustainability experts and the business units, thereby allowing the sustainability expertise to be available for supporting sustainability programs in the business units. The enhanced access for the sustainability directors also encourages and improves employee buy-in, although there is still no formal accountability and the actions of employees with respect to sustainability are largely determined by the priorities of the leaders of their specific business unit. In fact, the main problem with this structure is that responsibility and accountability remain dispersed; however, the structure can be helpful for companies with sustainability goals that are primarily focused on reducing costs and efficiency.

Another more advanced and dynamic structure for sustainability is referred to as an "embedded structure" and actually transfers the sustainability directors out of the sustainability function and into each of the business units and functions themselves. The sustainability director reports both to the leader of the business unit or function and back to the CSO—a matrix structure that can cause issues with respect to authority. For example, the director of sustainability procurement strategy would have reporting responsibilities to the vice president of procurement and the directors of environmental sustainability and sustainability communications would be reporting to the vice presidents of operations and PR/communications, respectively. Advantages of the embedded structure include the ability to select and implement sustainability programs that drive business value and become part of the company's core business and the opportunities to encourage significant buy-in from all employees. However, the embedded structure makes it more difficult for the CSO to coordinate sustainability activities across the organization and efforts may be duplicated. The CSO also has less management control and will have to depend more on his or her soft skills of influence and encouragement in order to make a significant impact. An embedded structure is considered to be the most advanced of the basic structures for sustainability and generally makes sense for mature organizations that have a good basic understanding of sustainability already integrated into their business units and are looking for revenue-generating opportunities.

Regardless of the particular structure adopted by an organization to facilitate its sustainability initiatives, it is essential to have executive sponsorship and visible and proactive support from the CEO and other members of the executive team and the board of directors. The CSO or other leader of the sustainability initiative must also establish relationships with the business and relevant functions in all of the company divisions and organizational units such as health, safety and environment; ethics and compliance; legal; product development; manufacturing; public affairs; marketing and communications; human resources and procurement. As companies grow larger, the CSO will have an entire sustainability leadership team to assist in sustainability oversight and coordination. For example, as mentioned above a company may create directorships for specific sustainability topics such as philanthropy; sustainability strategy and stakeholder engagement; EH&S and business continuity; communications and reporting; social business and special projects. The activities under each of the directorships may be supported by steering committees and other processes for coordination and collaboration.

The efforts of the CSO will often be supported by a "sustainability board" that includes representatives from all relevant functions and divisions and is dedicated to ensuring that sustainability activities are directed, guided and coordinated across the company and that duplication is minimized, results are reported and best practices are quickly shared. The sustainability board should have its own charter that describes the board's responsibilities and composition. For example, the board might be assigned responsibility for approving and/or recommending to the CSR committee of the board (and ultimately the entire board) an overall sustainability strategy, sustainability targets, sustainability policies, external sustainability positions, sustainability materiality assessment, sustainability communication and reporting approach, sustainability stakeholder engagement plan and major ESG index submissions. The sustainability board may also convene sustainability dialogue sessions with external stakeholders on the sustainability topics that are most material to the company's business, develop reports for internal and external use and ensure that information regarding sustainability activities is shared throughout the organization. The role of the board is to be particularly mindful of the cross-divisional/cross-functional implications of sustainability activities and thus it is important for the board to include the leaders of all business and functional units. The CSO or other sustainability leader should chair the sustainability board and one or more directors from the board-level CSR committee should have ex-officio participation rights. The board should meet no less frequently than quarterly and should be adequately supported by specialists working with the company's dedicated sustainability group or unit.

Sustainability Executives

Today the best practice is to have sustainability represented in the C-suite as a catalyst for the strong leadership and support for sustainability initiatives that must emanate from the senior executive team in order for those initiatives to capture the imagination and energy of employees and other stakeholders. The CSO should be sure that sustainability is taken into account when business strategy is being discussed and established in the boardroom and in meetings among senior executives, and should take the lead in communicating with operations managers about how budgets and performance metrics for particular programs have been established taking into account sustainability priorities. The CSO should also join the CEO in engaging with stakeholder groups to explain the company's sustainability strategy and obtain feedback and address concerns. Finally, the CSO should be responsible for ensuring that the company adheres to the continuous process of auditing and evaluating its sustainability activities in order to ensure that its sustainability strategies are coherent and effective.[10]

A guide prepared and distributed by the National Association of Corporate Directors looked at the role of the CSO position from the perspectives of the members of the company's board of directors and listed the following as core duties and responsibilities of the position:[11]

- ***Strategy:*** Lead development of an overarching sustainability approach directly related to the company's long-term business plans
- ***Thought Leadership:*** Broaden and raise the company's understanding of what society, customers, employees, investors and other stakeholders expect
- ***Advocacy:*** Speak out on behalf of the company's sustainability goals and accomplishments
- ***Policies and Programs:*** Drive the development and execution of guiding principles and initiatives for the company's sustainability programs
- ***Goals and Measurement:*** Develop appropriate targets and ways of assessing progress to drive and evaluate the company's performance on sustainability
- ***Reporting:*** Determine how the company will internally and externally express progress toward accomplishing its sustainability goals and respond to society's increasing demand for greater transparency
- ***Stakeholder Engagement:*** Build constructive alliances and coalitions with key constituency groups
- ***Risk Management:*** Identify risks and opportunities based on stakeholder expectations and design proactive mitigation and response strategies
- ***Fiscal Oversight:*** Through the sustainability strategic and operational planning process, develop an understanding of the fiscal impact of the company's goals and priorities in this area

As mentioned above, the preferred approach, assuming there are sufficient resources, is for the CSO position to be supported by a full sustainability leadership team with cross-functional experiences and skills drawn from key areas including corporate communications, operations, human resources, legal and compliance, sales, marketing, philanthropy, community relations and EH&S. As a practical matter, the size of the sustainability leadership team will be determined by factors that are beyond the control of the CSO including the size of the organization, responsibilities assigned to other functional areas and available capital and human resources. Surveys among even the largest organizations find that the CSO generally has to get by with a relatively small number of direct reports and a modest budget, which means that the CSO has to be adept at using their interpersonal skills to develop and maintain cooperative relationships with other parts of the company. In a series of reports on the evolution of the CSO, the Weinreb Group found that CSOs thrived and achieved success when they were able to build and manage multiple teams, and empower sustainability leaders, throughout the organization.[12]

One important sustainability leadership post is the vice president of sustainability, a senior operational role reporting to the CSO and responsible for oversight of the development and implementation of sustainability strategy and managing a team of sustainability specialist experts.[13] Inside the company the vice president of sustainability would work closely with executive leadership, the committee(s) of the board to which sustainability duties and activities have been assigned, business line managers (i.e., supply chain, human resources and environmental affairs), investor relations and governmental affairs and his or her direct reports. Facing outward, he or she would be working with community groups, NGOs and policy makers; media, financial and industry analysts; professional corporate responsibility organizations and peer counterparts. The required knowledge base and skill set for this position is not quite as broad as for the CSO position; however, he or she must have knowledge of economic, social and environmental sustainability and ethics and have a keen understanding of business conditions in the company's industry and the tools necessary for effective strategy execution and performance and risk management.

As one gets deeper into the staffing of the sustainability function, variations will necessarily be observed given that each organization has its own priorities and resources. As a point of reference regarding the specialist positions that might be created, consideration might be given to five other key sustainability-related positions within the organizational hierarchy mentioned by the Corporate Responsibility Officers Association:[14]

- *Director of Sustainability Communications:* Responsible for developing and executing a comprehensive, cohesive communications strategy for both internal and external audiences and for the production of the annual sustainability report, and uses the communications strategy to connect and convey broader reputation and social issues to the commercial objectives of the business. Works closely with internal groups like public relations, human resources, government affairs, investor relations, and environmental health and safety as well as with external stakeholders like SRIs, NGOs, customers, etc. The Director of Sustainability Communications plans, develops and leads the execution of a global sustainability communications plan, aligned with the company's sustainability goals. Candidates should have knowledge about stakeholder engagement and ethics and be skilled in change management, communications and risk management.
- *Director, Philanthropy:* This position is responsible for establishing, leading and managing a non-profit charitable foundation that awards grants annually to a variety of organizations in communities where

the company does business. Duties and responsibilities include overall strategic planning, revenue generation, financial management, organizational development, staff management and program operations. Candidates should have knowledge about social sustainability and ethics and be skilled in communications and strategy development and execution.

- *Director, Sustainability Procurement Strategy:* This position is a specialist procurement role focused on sustainability and includes developing and implementing procurement's strategy and policy on sustainability in relation to suppliers and their supply chains. Candidates should have knowledge about economic, social and environmental sustainability and ethics and be skilled in strategy execution, performance management and understanding the specific business elements of the industry in which the company operates.
- *Director of Environment, Health and Safety:* This position leads and directs the organization's EH&S processes and has company-wide responsibility for all EH&S related functions with accountability for operational, administrative, technical and financial components. Contributes to the development and execution of functional business plans and EH&S strategies and assesses operational risks that could affect EH&S in order to advise senior leadership on constructive plans and mitigation strategies. Candidates should have knowledge about environmental sustainability, stakeholder engagement and ethics and be skilled in strategy development and execution and risk management.
- *Director, Sustainability:* This position is responsible for developing a comprehensive sustainability strategy across all dimensions of sustainability that can be delivered through the tools of the practitioner, including issue monitoring, stakeholder consultation, materiality, risk analysis, transparency and reporting.

Management Systems

A management system refers to what an organization does to manage its structures, processes, activities and resources in order that its products or services meet the organization's objectives, such as satisfying the customer's quality requirements, complying with regulations and/or meeting environmental objectives. Elements of a management system include policy, planning, implementation and operations, performance assessment, improvement and management review. By systemizing the way it does things, an organization can increase efficiency and effectiveness, make sure that nothing important is left out of the process and ensure that everyone is clear about who is responsible for doing what, when, how, why and where. While all organizations should benefit from some form of management system, they are particularly important for larger organizations or ones with complicated processes. Management systems have been used for a number of years in sectors such as aerospace, automobiles, defense and health care.

Organizations implement management systems for a variety of reasons such as achieving business objectives, increasing understanding of current operations and the likely impact of change, communicating knowledge, demonstrating compliance with legal requirements and/ or industry standards, establishing "best practice", ensuring consistency, setting priorities or changing behavior.[15] Organizations often have more than one management system to deal with different activities or assets and integrate several related operational areas. For example, a customer relationship management system might be launched to manage relationships with customers. A preventive maintenance management and financial management systems may be used to preserve the value of organizational assets and human resource management systems merge and integrate the principles of human resource management with information technology. Other management systems focus on managing all relevant areas of operation in relation to a specific aspect such as quality, EH&S, information technology, data security, CSR, risk management and business continuity.

Even though they may not realize it, all organizations have some sort of management system–"the way things get done"—in place. Elements of the system may be documented in the form of policies and checklists, but much of the system is based on unwritten rules and customs. The interest of organizational leaders in management systems is based not only on the desire to understand how things are currently done but also to find out how "things should be done" in order to improve organizational performance. Fortunately, reference can be made to management system standards, such as those promulgated by the International Organization for Standardization (ISO) (www.iso.org), which are intended to provide all organizations with easy access to international "state-of-the-art" models that they can follow in implementing their own management systems. Management systems standards are concerned with processes, meaning the way that organizations go about carrying out their required work—they are not product and service standards, although processes certainly impact the quality of the organization's final products and services.

Many of the ISO standards are intended to be generic, which means that they can be applied to any organization, large or small, whatever its product or service; in any sector of activity; and whether it is a business enterprise, a public administration or a government department. The standards specify the requirements for a management system (e.g., objectives, policy, planning, implementation and operation, performance assessment, improvement and management review); however, the actual format of the system must be determined by the organization itself taking into account its specific goals and the environment in which it operates. ISO standards are available for management systems covering a broad range of topics including quality (ISO 9001), environment (ISO 14001), medical device quality (ISO 13485), medical device risk (ISO 14971), information security (ISO 27001 and ISO 27002), business continuity (ISO 22301), supply chain security (ISO 28000), corporate risk (ISO 31000), food safety (ISO 22000) and management auditing (ISO 19011).[16]

Implementing any management system, regardless of the system's particular focus (e.g., quality, environment, risk etc.), is a challenging task. In many cases, reference can be made to published management systems standards available from ISO and others; however, there are certain key activities that should always be considered:

- Identifying and understanding the organizational context
- Ensuring that senior management provides leadership in developing and implementing the system
- Developing a plan for the system that incorporates the risks and opportunities that could influence the performance of the system
- Ensuring that the organization is committed to support the system with the necessary internal and external resources
- Developing, planning, documenting, implementing and controlling the organization's operational processes
- Planning in advance for monitoring, measuring, analyzing and evaluating the performance of the system

An illustration of how a sustainability-focused management system might be designed and implemented was provided by Castka et al., who described a corporate social responsibility/Corporate Governance (CSR/CG) management system intended to be compatible with other management system standards, particularly ISO 9001 and ISO 14001.[17] The key elements of their system include defining the organization's CSR/CG policy; identifying the expectations of stakeholders; identifying and evaluating the organization's environmental and social impacts and risks; strategic planning and establishing the organization's CSR/CG objectives, targets and indicators; establishing and discharging the responsibilities of the board of directors and senior management with respect to managing the system; disclosure and reporting activities; monitoring, measuring and analyzing the processes included in the system; and managing change and ensuring continual improvement of the system.

Organizations may, and often do, seek and obtain certification by independent outside parties that their management systems conform to the requirements of ISO standards. In lieu of certification, or in preparation for a certification audit, organizations should conduct formal self-assessments on a regular basis that cover quality management system requirements; management responsibility requirements; resource management requirements; product realization requirements (e.g., planning, determination of customer requirements, design and development, purchasing, production and service provision); and measurement, analysis and improvement requirements.[18]

Role of the Legal Department

The legal department, particularly the general counsel, has a significant role to play in developing and implementing the CSR and sustainability initiatives of any organization. While CSR is often described as "going beyond the law", a good deal of the work relating to social and environmental responsibility involves understanding how to comply with existing laws and regulations and planning for and addressing the risks of misbehaviors in areas generally associated with CSR and sustainability such as human rights and child labor issues in the supply chain, discrimination in the workplace, health and safety issues, environmental practices, and cybersecurity and privacy. The legal department is also a natural contributor to organizational efforts to comply with voluntary standards, some of which will inevitably become hard law, and an experience guide on questions of materiality that arise as organizations expand their disclosure and reporting activities to include social and environmental goals and performance.

Notes

1 For discussion of board oversight of sustainability and establishing an effective board oversight framework, see Chapter 3 (Board Oversight of Sustainability) in this volume.
2 *CEOs and the New CSR Priority* (Boyden Executive Monitor, September 2017), available at www.boyden.com/media/ceos-and-the-new-csr-priority-2909935/index.html.
3 *A New Agenda for the Board of Directors: Adoption and Oversight of Corporate Sustainability* (Global Compact LEAD, 2012), 8.
4 Id. While the discussion in this section focuses on compensation and sustainability incentives for the CEO and other senior executives, the board should also ensure that incentives and related performance indicators and measurement systems are in place for all employees with responsibilities that link to the sustainability performance of the company and such incentives are aligned with those that have been established for senior executives. Id. at 9.
5 Id. There is also the option of providing, as is the case in certain extractive industries and the pharmaceutical industry, or of using "negative criteria" that is embedded in bonus rules that provide that no bonuses will be paid when incidents of a certain magnitude have occurred. Id. at 8–9.
6 Id. at 9.
7 D. Sampselle, *Sustainable Organization Design Principles*, OTMT 608.13, available at www.brevolutionconsulting.com/assets/Sustainable-Organization-Design-Principles.pdf (accessed May 12, 2020).
8 Id. at 8.

9   The discussion in this paragraph and the following paragraphs regarding alternative organizational structures for sustainability is adapted from H. Farr, Organizational Structure for Sustainability (July 14, 2011), http://abettercity. org/docs/events/BCBS%20Hayley%20Farr_28%20July%202011.pdf (accessed May 12, 2020).

10 K. Rangan, L. Chase and S. Karim, *Why Every Company Needs a CSR Strategy and How to Build It* (Cambridge MA: Harvard Business School Working Paper 12–088, April 5, 2012), 21–22 (while the term "CSO" is used in the text, Rangan et al. preferred to refer to the position as "Chief Responsibility Officer" and focused on strategic management of corporate social responsibility).

11 *C-SUITE EXPECTATIONS: Understanding C-Suite Roles Beyond the Core* (Washington DC: National Association of Corporate Directors, 2013).

12 *CSO Back Story: How Chief Sustainability Officers Reached the C-Suite* (Weinreb Group, September 2011) and *CSO Back Story II: The Evolution of the Chief Sustainability Officer* (Weinreb Group, Fall 2014).

13 Corporate Responsibility Officers Association, *Structuring and Staffing Corporate Responsibility: A Guidebook* (2010), 24.

14 Id. at 28–29.

15 A. Fraser, *Management Systems*, available at www.thecqi.org/Knowledge-Hub/Knowledge-portal/Corporate-strategy/Management-systems/ (accessed May 12, 2020).

16 For further discussion of designing and implementing sustainability-related management systems, see A. Gutterman, *Sustainability Management* (New York: Routledge, 2020).

17 P. Castka, C. Bamber and J. Sharp, *Implementing Effective Corporate Social Responsibility and Corporate Governance: A Framework* (British Standards Institution and the High Performance Organization Ltd., 2005).

18 See http://cw.routledge.com/textbooks/eresources/9781856176842/Requirement_checklist.pdf (accessed May 12, 2020).

13 Social Enterprises

For a long time, a significant potential impediment for sustainability initiatives that required investment of resources in activities that may appear to be unrelated to the traditional focus of U.S. corporations on maximizing profits for the stockholders was the fiduciary duties of the directors of the corporation. For example, when Henry Ford proposed to use surplus profits to hire additional employees to fight unemployment and increase benefits for employees rather than distribute such profits to the stockholders of Ford Motors, the Michigan Supreme Court, writing in 1919, found that Ford's actions would breach his fiduciary duty of good faith to the corporation.[1] The Court explained:

> A business corporation is organized and carried on primarily for the profit of the stockholders. The powers of the directors are to be employed for that end. The discretion of directors is to be exercised in the choice of means to attain that end, and does not extend to a change in the end itself, to the reduction of profits, or to the non-distribution of profits among stockholders in order to devote them to other purposes.

The Court also made it clear that "it is not within the lawful powers of a board of directors to shape and conduct the affairs of a corporation for the merely incidental benefit of shareholders and for the primary purpose of benefiting others".[2]

The fiduciary duties laid out in cases such as the one described above complicated efforts of directors to authorize sustainability initiatives that, by their very nature, are intended to create benefits for stakeholders other than stockholders that may well adversely impact stockholder value, at least in the short term, and deprive stockholders of distributions of surplus profits. However, as time has gone by, support has developed and increased for what Hart and Zingales referred to as the "constituency theory" of governance, which would expand the beneficiaries of the directors' fiduciary duties beyond shareholders to other constituencies, or stakeholders, such as employees, customers, members of the local communities in which the corporation operates and society as a whole.[3] While sentiment for encouraging long-termism and promoting a broader range of stakeholder interests has been around in some form for decades, the attacks on the primacy of shareholder value creation have never been as strident and are likely to accelerate in the future and become a permanent fixture among governance issues.

Compelling evidence of the desire to free directors of historical constraints, and thus promote more aggressive and entrepreneurial sustainability efforts, has been the decision of politicians in a majority of the states in the U.S. and the District of Columbia to endorse and formalize the constituency theory by adopting statutes that permit the formation of "benefit corporations", a new form of for-profit corporation that explicitly expands the fiduciary duties of directors beyond maximizing shareholder value, which is still one of the primary goals of a corporation, to include consideration of whether or not the corporation's activities have an overall positive impact on society, their workers, the communities in which they operate and the environment.[4] While the rate of adoption of benefit corporation status has been slow, particularly among public companies, the recognition of benefit corporations has contributed to sharpened focus on the separate interests of non-shareholder stakeholders and created a host of new issues and challenges for directors of all types of corporations such as how to measure and compare non-financial performance aspects of corporate activities; how to hold corporations accountable to stakeholders who do not have the rights to vote that are held by shareholders; and how to structure incentive packages for executives and managers tied to complex multi-stakeholder goals and commitments.

Benefit Corporations

A White Paper issued in 2013 by the Corporate Laws Committee of the Business Law Section of the American Bar Association (ABA White Paper) reported that since 2010 a number of U.S. jurisdictions had adopted provisions "allowing corporations to opt in to a legal structure that expressly expands the purpose of the corporation beyond advancing the pecuniary interests of its shareholders" and that would "allow or require directors to consider environmental, societal, or other impacts of corporate activity, even at the expense of shareholder value".[5] Corporations adopting these provisions are generally known as "benefit corporations" and the ABA White Paper noted that the first benefit corporation statutes were typically based on, or heavily influenced by, the Model Benefit Corporation Legislation (MBCL) drafted for B Lab Company (B Lab), a Pennsylvania non-profit corporation that has been described as "the driving force behind the adoption of benefit corporation legislation across the country".[6] The ABA White Paper went on to describe B Lab-based legislation as follows:[7]

In general, the legislation requires that a benefit corporation's charter confirm that it is obligated to pursue a general public benefit, creating a positive impact on society and the environment as a whole, as assessed against a third party standard. The legislation also permits the creation of specific public benefits in addition to the general benefit requirement. In making decisions, directors must consider the constituencies relevant to the general public benefit. In addition, the model legislation allows charter provisions that permit consideration of additional constituencies; however, the model legislation allows the board to prioritize those constituencies' interests, as long as it considers all of them.

The model legislation also requires that the corporation publish a "benefit report" to be made available to its shareholders each year. The report must measure the corporation's benefit performance against a third party standard. The definition of third party standard is very detailed. The B Lab Model also includes a specific rule for a "benefit director" who must opine as to the success of the corporation in acting in accordance with its general public purpose and specific public purposes. The legislation authorizes the shareholders to pursue "benefit enforcement proceedings", which are suits over whether a corporation is pursuing or creating the intended general public or specific public benefits. The B Lab Model legislation does not permit charter provisions that are inconsistent with the B Lab provisions.

Maryland was the first state to adopt legislation recognizing a "benefit corporation", which the statute described as a "corporation formed to create a material positive impact on society; consider how decisions affect employees, community and the environment; and publicly report their social and environmental performance using established third-party standards".[8] In Maryland, a benefit corporation must create a "general public benefit", which was defined as a material, positive impact on society and the environment, as measured by a third party standard, through activities that promote a combination of specific public benefits including providing individuals or communities with beneficial products or services; promoting economic opportunity for individuals or communities beyond the creation of jobs in the normal course of business; preserving the environment; improving human health; promoting the arts, sciences or advancement of knowledge; and/or increasing the flow of capital to entities with a public benefit purpose.

When Delaware, the recognized leader in statutory and case law innovations in the area of corporate law, passed its statute in 2013 recognizing "public benefit corporations" in the Delaware General Corporation Law (DGCL), the Governor made the following observations:[9]

Delaware public benefit corporations will function like and enjoy all the same benefits as traditional Delaware corporations and they will have three unique features that make them potential game changers. These three features concern corporate purpose, accountability, and transparency.

Corporate Purpose: Delaware public benefit corporations will have a corporate purpose "to operate in a responsible and sustainable manner". In addition, to provide directors, stockholders, and ultimately the courts, some direction, they are also required to identify in their certificate of incorporation a specific public benefit purpose the corporation is obligated to pursue. The overarching language helps ensure that a public benefit corporation serves the best long term interests of society while it creates value for its stockholders. The requirement to identify a specific public benefit purpose gives managers, directors, stockholders, and the courts, important guidance to ensure accountability, while preserving flexibility for business leaders and their investors to choose the specific public benefit purpose they feel will drive the greatest total value creation.

Accountability: Unlike in traditional corporations, whose directors have the sole fiduciary duty to maximize stockholder value, directors of public benefit corporations are required to meet a tri-partite balancing requirement consistent with its public benefit purpose. Directors are required to balance "the pecuniary interest of stockholders, the best interests of those materially affected by the corporation's conduct, and the identified specific public benefit purpose."

Transparency: Delaware public benefit corporations are required to report on their overall social and environmental performance, giving stockholders important information that, particularly when reported against a third party standard, can mitigate risk and reduce transaction costs. Given the trend in public equity markets toward integrated ESG (Environmental, Social and Governance) reporting and the growing private equity market for direct impact investing, this increased transparency can help investors to aggregate capital more easily as they are able to communicate more effectively the impact, and not just the return, of their investments.

California is another state that has promoted the creation of benefit corporations. For many years that state has recognized consumer cooperative corporations, small business corporations and business and industrial corporations. Recently, however, the choices have been expanded to include two additional corporate entities: benefit corporations and social purpose corporations. In California, a "benefit corporation" may be formed for the purpose of creating general public benefit, defined as a material positive impact on society and the environment, taken as a whole, as assessed against a third party standard that satisfies certain requirements.[10] A benefit corporation may also identify one or more specific public benefits as an additional purpose of the corporation including, without limitation, providing low-income or underserved individuals or communities with beneficial products or services, promoting economic opportunity for individuals or communities beyond the creation of jobs in the ordinary course of business, preserving the environment and improving human health.

Directors of California benefit corporations are required to consider the impacts of any action or proposed action upon specified considerations including, among others, the shareholders and employees of the corporation, customers of the corporation who are beneficiaries of the general or specific public benefit purposes and the environment. In addition, directors of benefit corporations are allowed to consider the impacts of those actions on, among other things, the resources, intent and conduct of any person seeking to acquire control of the benefit corporation. California benefit corporations must prepare an annual benefit report which includes, among other things, a statement indicating whether, in the board's opinion, the benefit corporation failed to pursue its general public benefit and any specific public benefit, a description of the ways in which the benefit corporation pursued those benefits, the extent to which those benefits were created and the process and rationale for selecting the third party standard used to prepare the benefit reports.

Formation of Benefit Corporations

Once the decision has been made to select a benefit corporation as the entity for the proposed business, attention turns to the actual formation and organization of the corporation.[11] Each of the states that recognize benefit corporations have their own specific requirements and the laws of the state in which the corporation will be incorporated should be carefully reviewed. The MBCL has been the model for the provisions adopted by most states with respect to formation and governance of benefit corporations including the requirements for drafting, filing and amending the articles of incorporation. In most cases, the most efficient thing for the promoters of a new benefit corporation is to incorporate in the state where most of the operational activities associated with the corporation will be performed, assuming that state authorizes the formation of benefit corporations. This generally provides the corporation with more than enough flexibility and certainty with respect to governance issues since most corporation law statutes are being continuously updated to reflect new developments that are being integrated into the MBCL. It is possible, however, for the entity to be formed and operated under the laws of another state (e.g., Delaware) when it is believed that the benefit corporation laws of that state relating to governance issues may provide advantages that may not be available under the laws of the state where initial operational activities will occur.[12]

Articles of Incorporation

The primary source for the basic rules regarding the structure and governance of the corporation is the articles of incorporation, which is sometimes referred to as the certificate of incorporation. In fact, a corporation cannot come into existence unless and until the articles have been filed with the secretary of state in the state in which the corporation is to be "incorporated". Once the articles have been filed they can be amended as provided under the applicable state corporation laws, a process which generally requires approval by the board and the shareholders. Amendments are common to reflect the growth and maturation of the corporation, especially changes in the composition of the shareholder group and the use of different types of securities to raise capital for the business. In particular, the provisions in the articles for "public companies" will differ dramatically from those in the articles for a small corporation with a handful of shareholders who also serve as directors and officers.

Mandatory Provisions

In general, benefit corporations must comply with the same requirements as any other for-profit corporation with respect to the contents of the articles of incorporation, as well as any specific requirements that are unique to benefit corporations. State corporation laws require that certain "mandatory" provisions must be included in the articles for every type of for-profit corporation, including a benefit corporation, and this obviously provides a good starting point for the drafting process. Each state is different; however, provisions typically tapped as "mandatory" include the name of the corporation (which must include, following the name, words or letters such as "Benefit Corporation", "B.C." or "BC"), the purposes of the corporation (general and specific benefit purposes as provided in the applicable benefit corporation statute), the number of authorized shares and identification of any classes or series of shares, the address of the registered office of the corporation, the name of the registered agent of the corporation and the name and address of each incorporator. The registered agent of the corporation is usually one of the many commercial entities that provide such services to corporations and the name of the chosen agent and its office should be inserted into the articles once the agent has agreed to act on behalf of the corporation. In many cases, the agent can actually handle the filing of the articles once the drafting is completed. Certain states may have additional "mandatory" requirements that must be observed, including the need to specify the duration of existence for the corporation, which typically is "perpetual"; the location of the principal office of the corporation, as opposed to the registered office; and the names and addresses of the initial directors.

Purposes and Powers Provisions

The most important and distinguishing issue with respect to drafting the initial articles of incorporation for a benefit corporation is drafting the mandatory "purposes" provisions. In general, a benefit corporation can be formed with the purpose of engaging in any lawful purpose. The articles of incorporation may set forth a more limited purpose, perhaps in order to distinguish the corporation from other organizations and provide some guidelines for others who might work with the corporation in the future as to the initial purpose for the organization. In addition, the articles of incorporation should identify any restrictions or limitations on the corporation's activities or powers, and make a public statement of purpose, although the purpose should be general enough to allow the corporation to continue to operate in changing circumstances and broad enough to cover all the actual and planned activities of the corporation.

When Delaware, the recognized leader in statutory and case law innovations in the area of corporate law, recognized "public benefit corporations" in the DGCL, DGCL § 362(a) defined a "public benefit corporation" as a for-profit corporation organized under and subject to the requirements of the DGCL that is intended to produce a public benefit or public benefits and to operate in a responsible and sustainable manner.[13] The statute makes it clear that to that end, a public benefit corporation must be managed in a manner that balances the stockholders' pecuniary interests, the best interests of those materially affected by the corporation's conduct, and the public benefit or public benefits identified in its certificate of incorporation. DGCL § 362(b) defines "public benefit" to mean a positive effect (or reduction of negative effects) on one or more categories of persons, entities, communities or interests (other than stockholders in their capacities as stockholders) including, but not limited to, effects of an artistic, charitable, cultural, economic, educational, environmental, literary, medical, religious, scientific or technological nature.

DGCL § 362(b) has been construed as requiring that Delaware public benefit corporations should set out a specific public benefit in their certificate of incorporation; however, the statute does not provide explicit guidance as to how specific the public benefit needs to be. Commentators have recommended that Delaware public benefit corporations should pick a public benefit that is more narrowly defined than a restatement of the general benefit that the statute requires but which is still stated broadly enough to limit the need for future amendments to its certificate of incorporation when changes are made in the manner in which the corporation goes about achieving its purpose (e.g., a change in the method of providing nutritious meals by a benefit corporation formed to provided nutritious meals should not require an amendment to the certificate of incorporation).[14]

Optional Provisions

While articles containing the "mandatory" provisions discussed above are sufficient to "form" a new benefit corporation as a legal entity, the preparation of the articles is an opportunity to consider and address a wide range of corporate governance and financial issues by inclusion of so-called "optional" provisions. For example, depending on the circumstances, it may be appropriate to deviate from the statutory norm in drafting language relating to capital stock provisions, such as authorizing preferred shares with special rights, preferences and privileges to be issued to outside investors; shareholders' rights, actions and meetings; and officers and directors. Optional provisions are commonly used in situations where the corporation will have a small number of shareholders and has been formed to engage in a limited range of operational activities and the shareholders wish to be quite specific in the articles about the purpose of the corporation and the powers of the officers and directors to take actions in the name of the corporation.

One specific topic for optional provisions in the articles or certificate of incorporation concerns how the benefit corporation will satisfy its reporting obligations and its duties with respect to transparency to its stakeholders. Every benefit corporation will be subject to the reporting requirements set out in the statutes of the state in which it is incorporated and there generally is no need to restate those requirements in the articles or certificate of incorporation or bylaws; however, some corporations may opt to adhere to more stringent requirements and do so by formally integrating those requirements into their charter documents. For example, DGCL § 366 requires Delaware public benefit corporations to provide stockholders a biennial report assessing the corporation's promotion of its stated public benefit or benefits and describing the board's goals and standards regarding stakeholders; however, such corporation may elect to increase the level of transparency so that it is equivalent to the standard provided for in the MBCL by including option provisions in the certificate of corporation that obligate the corporation to prepare benefit reports annually, rather than biennially, make the report public and use a third party standard for the assessment included in the report.

Alternative U.S. Structures for Social Enterprises

While benefit corporations have attracted a significant amount of attention, there have been other attempts to create and popularize alternative business structures for social enterprise. For example, a "L3C", or "low-profit limited liability company", is a for-profit, social enterprise venture that has a stated goal of performing a socially beneficial purpose, not maximizing income, which has been recognized by statute in a handful of states and tribal nations. The first state to recognize the L3C was Vermont, which defined it to mean a limited liability company (LLC) organized for a business purpose that satisfies and is at all times operated to satisfy each of the following requirements: (A) the company significantly furthers the accomplishment of one or more charitable or educational purposes and would not have been formed but for the company's relationship to the accomplishment of charitable or educational purposes; and (B) no significant purpose of the company is the production of income or the appreciation of property; provided, however, that the fact that a person produces significant income or capital appreciation shall not, in the absence of other factors, be conclusive evidence of a significant purpose involving the production of income or the appreciation of property. Proponents of the L3C have touted the entity as embodying the operating efficiencies of a for-profit company along with a reduced regulatory structure. As an LLC, a L3C is able to bring together foundations, trusts, endowment funds, pension funds, individuals, corporations, other for-profits and government entities into an organization designed to achieve social objectives while also operating according to for-profit metrics. The L3C can also take advantage of the LLC structure to operate with the flexibility of membership and organization needed to cover a wide variety of social enterprise situations while including the liability protection of a corporation.[15]

Commentators have also suggested that the operating agreement of a traditional Delaware LLC may be drafted to create the same characteristics of purpose, accountability and transparency as benefit corporations.[16] When the business is being operated as a traditional for-profit corporation the charter documents may be drafted to give control over the socially responsible mission of the company to a single class of shareholders, thus providing members of that class with veto power over certain corporate acts that may be at odds with a specific sustainability-related purpose that is of importance to a significant number of shareholders. In lieu of provisions in the charter documents, shareholders and officers of a traditional for-profit corporation may enter into contractual agreements pertaining to the mission. Another method that might be used is a licensing arrangement wherein valuable intellectual property is held by a non-profit or the founders in order to preserve the mission through a protective license back to the company. Finally, many social entrepreneurs choose to formally organize their mission-based businesses as a non-profit corporation.

European Social Enterprises and Benefit Companies

It should come as no surprise that jurisdictions outside of the U.S. have also attempted to develop and/or otherwise support governance frameworks that might be suitable for sustainable entrepreneurs with interests that extend beyond profit-making. In Europe, for example, the European Commission launched a Social Business Initiative in 2011 that aimed to introduce a short-term action plan to support the development of social enterprises, key stakeholders in the social economy and social innovation.[17] The initial priorities of the Commission were organized around three themes: making it easier for social enterprises to obtain funding; increasing the visibility of social entrepreneurship; and making the legal environment friendlier for social enterprises. The Commission described "social enterprises" as follows:

A social enterprise is an operator in the social economy whose main objective is to have a social impact rather than make a profit for their owners or shareholders. It operates by providing goods and services for the market in an entrepreneurial and innovative fashion and uses its profits primarily to achieve social objectives. It is managed in an open and responsible manner and, in particular, involves employees, consumers and stakeholders affected by its commercial activities.

As opposed to U.S. benefit corporations, which are distinguishable legal entities, the social enterprise that the Commission has in mind does not follow a single legal form and the Commission noted that many social enterprises operate in the form of social cooperatives, some were registered as private companies limited by guarantee, some were mutual, and a lot of them were non-profit organizations such as voluntary organizations, charities or foundations. Regardless of form, social enterprises should be understood to include businesses for which the social or societal objective of the common good is the reason for the commercial activity, often in the form of a high level of social innovation; businesses in which profits are mainly reinvested to achieve this social objective; and businesses that have adopted a method of organization or ownership system that reflects the enterprise's mission, using democratic or participatory principles or focusing on social justice. Common fields of operation for social enterprises according to the Commission include work integration, personal social services, local development of disadvantaged areas, recycling, environmental protection, arts, culture or historical preservation, science, research and innovation and consumer protection.

An important trend to watch is the movement of the benefit corporation concept to Europe and the recognition of a European benefit corporation. The first steps were taken in Italy in December 2015 when the Italian parliament adopted the "Stability Act of 2016", which provided for the creation of a "Società Benefit", a separate legal entity formed and organized for the pursuit of one or more "common benefit" purposes as well as an economic activity. The move was notable for the fact that it was the first benefit corporation created in a civil law legal system and commentators have noted that while the new entity has many of the characteristics of U.S. benefit corporations, it was created in a completely different legal and social context given that directors in Italy and in other civil law countries were already allowed to take into consideration stakeholder interests and thus it was not necessary to be too concerned about protecting directors.[18]

The main objective of the European benefit corporation movement seems to be promoting a completely new model of conducting business that supports pursuit of both economic and social purposes simultaneously. The Stability Act describes a "Società Benefit" as a company that aims at the distribution of profits, but, at the same time, pursues one or more common benefit goals in favor of other stakeholders in the business, including people, communities, territories and the environment, cultural heritage, social activities, entities and associations, by working in a responsible, sustainable and transparent manner. Designation as a "Società Benefit" is available to any for-profit company and while the model has borrowed many of the main characteristics of a U.S. benefit corporation there are important differences: the "Società Benefit" must list in the bylaws the specific benefit activities; the annual report must be more detailed than the U.S. benefit corporation; directors are not eligible for limitation of their liabilities with respect to third party lawsuits and the scope of the law applies not only to for-profit companies, but also to limited-profit companies.[19]

Notes

1 D. Sampselle, *Sustainable Organization Design Principles*, OTMT 608.13. available at www.brevolutionconsulting.com/assets/Sustainable-Organization-Design-Principles.pdf (accessed May 12, 2020) 11.
2 Dodge v. Ford, 204 Mich. 459, 170 N.W. 668 (1919).
3 O. Hart and L. Zingales, "Should a Company Pursue Shareholder Value?" (October 2016), available at www8.gsb.columbia.edu/leadership/sites/leadership/files/Zingales-Hart–Share_value.pdf (accessed May 12, 2020).
4 By 2020, over forty states and the District of Columbia had either adopted legislation authorizing the creation of a benefit corporation or were seriously considering such legislation https://benefitcorp.net/policymakers/state-by-state-status.
5 Corporate Laws Committee of the ABA Business Law Section, "Benefit Corporation White Paper", *The Business Lawyer*, 68 (August 2013), 1083.
6 Id.
7 Id. at 1087–1088.
8 D. Sampselle, *Sustainable Organization Design Principles*, OTMT 608.13. available at www.brevolutionconsulting.com/assets/Sustainable-Organization-Design-Principles.pdf (accessed May 12, 2020), 12–13 (see Maryland Corporations and Associations Article §§ 5-6C-01 through -08).
9 J. Markell, "A New Kind of Corporation to Harness the Power of Private Enterprise for Public Benefit", *Huffington Post* (July 22, 2013), available at www.huffingtonpost.com/gov-jack-markell/public-benefit-corporation_b_3635752.html (accessed May 12, 2020). For a comprehensive guide to Delaware's public benefit corporation statute, see F. Alexander, *The Public Benefit Corporation Guidebook: Understanding and Optimizing Delaware's Benefit Corporation Governance Model* (Morris Nichols Arscht & Tunnell, 2016).
10 See Ca. Corp. Code §§ 14600 et seq.
11 While the discussion in this chapter is based on the assumption that the benefit corporation is being newly formed, it is also possible for an existing "traditional" corporation to convert to a benefit corporation while continuing to engage in the activities that were in place before the conversion.
12 In general, state statutes, although varying from case-to-case, address three major areas: corporate purpose (i.e., creating a material positive impact on

society and the environment); accountability (i.e. expanded fiduciary duties of directors that extend beyond shareholders to include consideration of non-financial interests); and transparency (i.e., an obligation to report on its overall social and environmental performance as assessed against a comprehensive, credible, independent and transparent third-party standard). The statutes in MBCL states (i.e., states with a benefit corporation statute modeled after the MBCL) are relatively similar; however, statutes adopted in influential states such as California and Delaware have departed from the MBCL in many ways.

13 DGCL § 362(a) requires public benefits corporations to identify in their certificate of incorporation within its statement of business or purpose one or more specific public benefits to be promoted by the corporation; and state within its heading that it is a public benefit corporation (such provisions are generally referred to as "public benefit provisions"). In addition to the provisions described herein, the DGCL also includes requirements relating to the name of public benefit corporations (DGCL § 362(c)), amendments to the certificate of incorporation and certain mergers involving public benefit corporations (DGCL § 363); and stock certificates and notices regarding uncertificated stock (DGCL § 364).

14 F. Alexander, E. Klinger-Wilensky and M. Divincenzo, "Certificate of Incorporation (DE): Public Benefit Corporation Provisions" (Thomson Reuters: Practical Law, 2016).

15 For additional information on the L3C, see the website of Americans for Community Development (https://americansforcommunitydevelopment.org/). See also M. Carreira da Cruz, "Legal Innovation and Social Entrepreneurship Formats", *American International Journal of Contemporary Research*, 2(10) (October 2012), 59 (discussing the L3C and efforts to create a new corporate format dedicated to social entrepreneurship in foreign countries such as Belgium, the United Kingdom and Luxemburg).

16 F. Alexander, E. Klinger-Wilensky and M. Divincenzo, "Certificate of Incorporation (DE): Public Benefit Corporation Provisions" (Thomson Reuters: Practical Law, 2016).

17 The discussion of "social enterprises" in this section is adapted from information appearing at http://ec.europa.eu/growth/sectors/social-economy/enterprises_en (accessed May 12, 2020).

18 A. Pelatan and R. Randazzo, *The First European Benefit Corporation: Blurring the Lines Between "Social" and "Business"*, available at www.bwbllp.com/file/benefit-corporation-article-june-16-pdf (accessed May 12, 2020).

19 Id.

Index

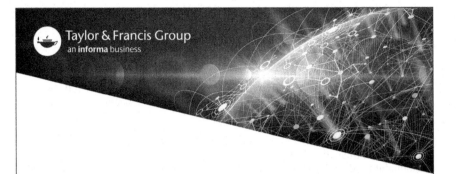

Printed in the United States
By Bookmasters